The Evolving Role of the Professional Support Lawyer

EDITED BY FRANCESCA RAMADAN

Commissioning editor
Alex Davies

Managing director
Sian O'Neill

The Evolving Role of the Professional Support Lawyer is published by

Globe Law and Business Ltd
3 Mylor Close
Horsell
Woking
Surrey GU21 4DD
United Kingdom
Tel: +44 20 3745 4770
www.globelawandbusiness.com

Printed and bound by CPI Group (UK) Ltd, Croydon CR0 4YY.

The Evolving Role of the Professional Support Lawyer

ISBN 9781783583485
EPUB ISBN 9781787427570
Adobe PDF ISBN 9781787427587

Contents

Contents

Executive summary

The role of the professional support lawyer (PSL) first emerged in the early- to mid-1990s amongst London's Magic Circle, and quickly became essential for mid-size and even smaller firms. However, this golden period for the PSL came to an abrupt end with the global financial crisis and the subsequent recession, which rocked the legal landscape; the greatest shockwaves were inevitably felt by legal support teams, as many firms sought to maintain profitability by shifting their focus to fee-earners and cutting what was quickly perceived as superfluous business functions. The slow but steady recovery of the economy and the consequent pick-up of client demand since then has meant that the importance of PSLs to law firm operations has once again been recognised.

However, the legal profession is not the same as it was before the recession; this is reflected in not only changes in what is expected from fee-earners, but also support staff such as PSLs. Traditionally seen as a backstage position that mainly involved administrative work and the drafting of precedents, the PSL role is rapidly transforming. A PSL now cannot only contribute to a firm's competitive edge by providing the traditional technical expertise. it has now become essential to perform tasks ranging from involvement in business development to the provision of training, the capture and dissemination of knowledge, product selection, and project management. This kind of flexibility is what has made the role of the PSL attractive to those seeking an alternative to legal practice; however, it brings its own challenges. With such a wide variety of responsibilities and functions, it can be difficult to find relevant information on what career development might look like, or the skills needed for the progression. Identifying current issues and future challenges, too, is rendered problematic by this versatility.

The Evolving Role of the PSL aims to fill this information gap. Featuring contributions from current PSLs, it provides up-to-the-minute intelligence from an insider's perspective on common issues and the solutions to tackle them. This is supplemented by advice from experts, ranging from knowledge management specialists to PSL recruiters, and compelling case studies that provide a crucial insight into real-world industry and career experience.

To discern potential paths that may open up for the PSL in the future, it is critical to examine the role's past. In chapter 1, Ailish Hogan and Lucinda Troostwyk – both experienced PSL recruiters at Taylor Root, one of the world's largest legal recruitment consultancies – explore the development of the PSL role, detailing its inception, its relationship to market conditions, and how perceptions are changing. Ailish and Lucinda proceed to then look forward, discussing the way in which career structure and progression prospects are transforming, shifting the role from a professional segue into a viable and freestanding career path of its own.

Many smaller firms find that they have been gaining PSLs over the years, but have not yet developed appropriately tailored career paths or competency frameworks. Instead, the role of the knowledge or support lawyers often develops ad-hoc, with no real reference to knowledge management theory and practice and how it ought to permeate the role and expectations of the PSL. In chapter 2, Hélène Russell – founder of TheKnowledgeBusiness – seeks to rectify this by looking at how a firm might develop these core competencies, harnessing the full potential of the PSL and enabling this valuable and expensive resource to achieve their return on investment.

One of the aspects of the role that PSLs often grapple with is how to demonstrate the value that they can bring. Although fee-earners who have the assistance of PSLs often see them as integral to the success of their team or department, in a sector where KPIs and fee targets are routinely used to measure performance and value, how can PSLs demonstrate the value they add in a tangible way? Drawing on her experience of developing the professional support role, Catherine Hart – partner and PSL at Digby Brown – outlines in chapter 3 the way in which this role has developed in Scotland and looks at some practical ways in which those providing professional support can demonstrate the value of the work that they undertake.

Assuming that a PSL has built a large body of specialist expertise through awareness of legislative priorities in their practice area and recent developments in case law, how can this be effectively leveraged to generate value for clients and the team? In chapter 4, Katherine Lang – senior PSL at Taylor Wessing – looks at the life-cycle of knowledge, and makes the case that this value can be created through the efficient use of generic and tailored knowledge products, the optimisation of those products for the relevant audience, and by a critical examination of the value of online content.

The concept of document automation is not new to the legal world, but surprisingly few firms have automated their precedents; most have yet to make the investment and take advantage of the step change offered in practice efficiency. As traditional gatekeepers for precedent banks, PSLs are a natural fit to contribute, oversee, or even project manage a firm or department's shift to automation. In chapter 5, Clare Harman Clark – senior PSL at Taylor Wessing – sets out the process for PSLs so tasked, taking in elements such as project establishment, product selection, and launch and implementation.

The PSL role can be shaped by a number of factors beyond those relating to either personal or business aspects, with larger societal changes and technological developments driving change in unexpected ways. Drawing from his long and comprehensive experience, in chapter 6, Charles Pigott – PSL at Mills & Reeve – outlines the ways in which his career has developed in response to economic conditions and legislative changes, in a fascinating case study that highlights the flexibility that PSLs must cultivate. This chapter also looks forward to upcoming seismic shifts in the legal landscape – namely, Brexit – and offers visions, based on past experience, of what the future might demand from PSLs.

The kind of flexibility illustrated in the previous chapter has its downsides, however, including negotiating the different type of activities that PSLs undertake, and managing time and priorities for each. In chapter 7, Karen Battersby – director of knowledge and learning and development at Charles Russell Speechlys – tackles this important issue, exploring the importance of managing fee-earner expectations and communicating priorities, as well as the benefits of having a clearly prioritised and articulated plan for different types of work. This is supplemented by practical workload and time management tips, offered as guidance for those seeking tools to assist with their prioritisation and planning.

There may be occasions in a PSL's career where the manifold tasks expected of them, alongside their considerable workload, may prove overwhelming. This could be the ideal time for a paralegal to be hired, offering additional support or providing specialist expertise for a particular project or period. However, the opinion that paralegals have no place amongst professional legal support staff remains widespread. In chapter 8, Amanda Hamilton – chief executive of the National Association of Licenced Paralegals – delves into how paralegals can benefit PSLs, outlining what tasks they can perform, in order to help you understand when a paralegal might be the solution and how to identify the perfect fit.

Artificial intelligence is continually evolving and is intertwined with the evolving role of the PSL, who is increasingly expected to participate in AI projects. Indeed, AI has become crucial to the role of the PSL, who needs to know what impact new technology products will have on legal documents and firm-wide process management. In chapter 9, Lucy Hall – senior PSL at Eversheds Sutherland – delves into AI development and its relationship with PSLs, as well as examining the range of products available to the legal industry. She also looks to the future to speculate on what form the relationship between PSLs and AI may take.

One of the ways in which the PSL role has transformed is in the relatively new development of active engagement in business development. In chapter 10, Julia Bateman – PSL at Kingsley Napley – examines the relationship and value of "horizon scanning" in terms of using current awareness to build fee-earner profile. She discusses how long-term awareness of legislative projects and political priorities can be used to demonstrate thought leadership and expertise to clients, drawing from examples from her own firm to offer insight informed by essential real-world experience.

PSLs have been a staple in UK law firms for over two decades, but their penetration into the US legal space is a far more recent phenomenon. In chapter 11, Evan Shenkman – director of KM counsel and research at US-based Ogletree Deakins – transitioned from shareholder to PSL in 2011, becoming the first in Ogletree's then nascent KM department. While growing the firm's PSL team over the next seven years, as well as co-chairing the New York City PSL Network, Evan obtained unique insights into the state of PSLs in the US. His chapter includes a discussion of the role of PSLs in the United States, the growth of the industry, and how he sees the PSL's responsibilities shifting in the years to come.

About the authors

Julia Bateman joined the team as a professional support lawyer at Kingsley Napley, the leading criminal defence firm in the UK, in July 2015. She is responsible for knowledge management and "know-how"/current awareness development for the criminal litigation team (including business and financial crime, general crime, and EU/international). She has a particular expertise in European criminal justice, having started her career in this area with a traineeship in the European Commission. From 2001-2003, she worked at the European Parliament as political advisor and was the first to hold the post of justice and home affairs policy advisor. She was head of office from 2008 and returned to the Law Society headquarters in London as head of international in 2011. She is a non-practising barrister.

Karen Battersby is the head of knowledge and learning and development at Charles Russell Speechlys, and is responsible for the firm's knowledge management, library, and learning and development departments. She has many years' experience in knowledge management, as well as a commercial lawyer, having practised both in private practice and in-house. Karen is an experienced lecturer and trainer, having taught everything from legal CPD courses to MBA qualifications to lawyers and other professionals. She established the UK's first postgraduate qualification in knowledge management for legal practice at Nottingham Law School. Karen also developed one of the first webinar and online learning businesses for the legal profession.

Lucy Hall is the sole senior associate professional support lawyer for the banking team at Eversheds Sutherland in London. She supports over 100 banking fee earners in the UK and internationally, and specialises in corporate finance, project finance, and real estate finance. Lucy is responsible for writing and delivering training, collating know-how, keeping the team up to date with legal and technical developments, as well as creating and maintaining precedents. She was previously a senior professional support lawyer in the finance groups at Hogan Lovells and Mayer Brown, having previously qualified and worked as a fee earner for almost eight years.

Amanda Hamilton is chief executive of the National Association of Licenced Paralegals (NALP), a non-profit membership body and the only paralegal body recognised as an awarding organisation by Ofqual (the regulator of qualifications in England). Through its training arm, NALP Training, accredited recognised professional paralegal qualifications are offered for a career as a paralegal professional.

Clare Harman Clark is a senior professional support lawyer at Taylor Wessing LLP, building on a legal career that began with nearly a decade at Clifford Chance and a stint at Russell Cooke. Before retaining as a lawyer, Clare worked as a journalist and within a government press office, and still regularly publishes articles in national and trade press.

Catherine Hart graduated from Glasgow University and has over 25 years' experience in civil litigation, mainly in the field of personal injury. Catherine has worked in professional support for 11 years and has experience of setting up and establishing the PSL role in two law firms. She joined Digby Brown in 2014 and became a partner in 2017. Along with a team, Catherine supports fee earners in all the firm's offices across Scotland. As well as the more traditional aspects of professional support, Catherine's role has developed into areas of management, including risk management and regulation. Catherine is a passionate advocate of the professional support role. She has written articles and delivered talks on the importance of the role and the value that PSLs can bring.

Ailish Hogan qualified as a solicitor in 2002 and spent four years specialising in corporate finance before joining Taylor Root, a legal recruitment consultancy, in January 2007. Together with her colleague Lucinda – and their collective 20 years recruiting for private practice firms at Taylor Root – she established a dedicated PSL team. They now focus on recruiting professional support lawyers and knowledge managers into a range of City, niche and West End law firms, and work with a wide spectrum of candidates, from those wishing to make their first move into a PSL role to experienced PSLs considering new opportunities.

Katherine Lang is a senior professional support lawyer in the real estate team at Taylor Wessing LLP. As a PSL, Katherine advises on complex transactional and structuring points, provides legal training, maintains the team's bank of precedent documents, and keeps the team and clients abreast of legal developments and their business impact. She has written articles for legal and trade publications such as *Estates Gazette*, *Property Week*, *Construction Week*, and *LexisPSL*. Prior to joining Taylor Wessing, Katherine was a transactional lawyer at Norton Rose Fulbright LLP for thirteen years. She graduated from the University of Oxford in 2001.

Charles Pigott has been a professional support lawyer in Mills & Reeve's employment, immigration and pensions team since 2001. He trained in the City and – before joining Mills & Reeve – worked as a partner in a large London legal aid practice. His main responsibility is to help the firm deliver a better service to its employment clients, collaborating with colleagues across the business. Charles currently edits the Mills & Reeve employment blog "hrlawlive" and the firm's Brexit hub. He also writes regularly for the *New Law Journal* on employment topics.

Hélène Russell of TheKnowledgeBusiness is a lawyer (non-practising) and specialist in knowledge management. She has worked as a self-employed KM'er since 2008, and specialises in translating complex academic thought leadership and cross-boundary theories into practical tools to improve the efficiency and profitability of law firms. Hélène is the author of *Knowledge Management Handbook* (2012) and *Practical Projects in Legal KM* (2015), as well as several chapters for ARK's multi-contributor books. She is a frequent conference speaker and runs regular open KM training events, as well as overseeing nationwide KM community groups. Hélène has completed an executive MBA with distinction, with a focus on antecedents to knowledge sharing within UK law firms.

Evan J Shenkman helps firm attorneys work smarter, faster, and more in sync; creates internal and client-facing collaborative tools; and manages his firm's PSLs and legal researchers. Past projects include development of his firm's enterprise search tool (ODSearch), their SharePoint intranet (ODConnect), their agency charge tool (IntelliCase), and a vast array of firm AI and analytics tools. He also manages the firm's KM Legal Resources Center, a SharePoint home for the firm's vetted model documents, practice guides, links, and subject matter experts, and its 50-state survey collection. In his spare time, Evan is co-chair of the NYC Practice Support Lawyers Network, presents at ARK and ILTA conferences, and coaches travel soccer teams.

Lucinda Troostwyck read law at Birmingham University and qualified as a corporate solicitor in 2005 before joining Taylor Root, a legal recruitment consultancy, in 2006. Together with her colleague Ailish – and their collective 20 years recruiting for private practice firms at Taylor Root – she established a dedicated PSL team. They now focus on recruiting professional support lawyers and knowledge managers into a range of City, niche and West End law firms, and work with a wide spectrum of candidates, from those wishing to make their first move into a PSL role to experienced PSLs considering new opportunities.

Chapter 1:
The evolving role of the PSL – past, present and future

By Ailish Hogan and Lucinda Troostwyck, PSL and KM recruitment specialists at Taylor Root

Background

Traditionally, professional support lawyers were a function of large City firms, providing and updating a central precedent bank, conducting research, and delivering internal training. Following the economic downturn in 2008, PSLs were suddenly considered a luxury, and many were made redundant. From 2013 onwards, the PSL market began to recover, and the role was re-established in many firms, albeit transformed from its previous guise. Now, at a growing number of firms, the PSL function is seen as a fundamental part of the business infrastructure and a critical contribution to both internal and – increasingly – external efficiency and productivity. The profile of the role has undoubtedly been raised, with real importance now being attached to its function.

As the PSL role has developed, the job title has too been adapted. This chapter refers to the role of the "PSL", but these developments apply to a wider range of roles, including knowledge development lawyers, KM attorneys and practice development lawyers – a reflection that the position has genuinely evolved beyond that of a support function.

How has the role of the PSL evolved?

Previously, PSLs would work reactively to fee-earners' enquiries and their needs for training. Increasingly, the role of the PSL requires a much more proactive approach. Rather than just preparing and delivering internal training, PSLs will work as part of a wider KM function to identify and efficiently develop the training strategy of the firm. Larger projects and strategic initiatives relating to the KM function will be part of their remit, whilst continuing to deal with day-to-day enquiries.

A key part of the PSL role is now to encourage fee-earners to re-think their approach to KM, and to ensure that processes around knowledge sharing are in place and observed. The PSL will frequently now form an essential part of a well-structured knowledge management team, saving the fee-earners time and increasing productivity by enabling them to focus on billing. There is also an increasing degree of interaction for a PSL with other teams in the business (e.g. marketing, business development, IT), and what was predominantly an internal facing role is becoming more client-focused. A strong and highly responsive KM team – of which the PSL frequently forms an integral part – ensures knowledge is consistent, shared, and constantly evolving with the business to meet clients' needs and demands.

More than ever, PSLs are able to develop and shape their own role; partners and group heads are now encouraging PSLs to carve out their ideal job and are always interested in new areas of expertise and innovative concepts. As the scope of the PSL role has expanded, some of the larger PSL teams now have their own support team in place – knowledge paralegals and knowledge and information officers, for example, are becoming more common.

The last couple of years have seen a noticeable increase in newly created positions. Titles vary, but the premise is the same: to ensure that teams across the firm collaborate and have a shared commitment to the PSL function. There has been a genuine shift from the PSL as purely a support role to existing as a vital part of a law firm's infrastructure.

The range of roles now on offer, from entry-level PSL to global head of knowledge, makes this area a genuinely attractive alternative to fee-earning.

How have internal perceptions changed?

Previously, the role of a PSL was largely standalone, with little interaction with members of the firm outside the specific practice group. Now, however, PSLs are much more integral to the wider firm. Experienced PSLs will often report into partners and group heads and will be consulted on wider knowledge management issues and strategies. PSLs are now commonly working with internal marketing, business development and IT teams and are pivotal in bringing these elements of the firm's infrastructure together cohesively. A former candidate of ours has observed:

> *"Eight years ago [in my role as a corporate PSL], I rarely worked with anyone outside my immediate team. It was probably the only thing I missed about being a fee-earner! Now, our internal network of PSLs have expanded so I have a great peer group and on a daily basis I'm working with other teams in the firm. I'm really enjoying being such an integral part of the firm, and its been great for raising my profile internally."*

What about external attitudes?

PSLs are now expected to be more client-facing than ever and are becoming a valuable resource for clients too. Preparing clients updates on legislative and regulatory changes has long been a part of the role, but most PSLs are now enjoying increased access to clients. Many will now provide training to large FTSE clients on key areas of law. One client of ours has stated:

> *"Twice a year our employment PSL attends our [global banking] client's office to provide updates on recent legislation and market practice. Having an expert who can go in and explain complex legislation and, importantly, its impact in a commercial context – which allows [the client] to avoid pitfalls – has been invaluable."*

Being an expert on the black letter of the law has always been a pre-requisite, but there is now a growing trend for experienced PSLs to be involved in responses to legislative consultations. The level of contributions by PSLs to articles, journals and publications as experts in their field is also increasing, with experienced PSLs regularly being asked to contribute on issues around knowledge strategy.

What are the challenges?

As the scope of the PSL role has evolved, so too have the challenges faced. Recent advances in technology and the pressure to reduce costs mean that PSLs are now required to keep up-to-date with technological advances, and are increasingly working with IT teams to provide a framework for knowledge management. Becoming a PSL remains an attractive option for many fee-earners, and for good reason. However, in practice areas where PSL roles are scarce (real estate, disputes, employment and tax), competition is often fierce. Those wishing to make the move, particularly at entry level, will need to upskill and expand their capabilities. As well as academic and technical excellence, fee-earners need to demonstrate genuine enthusiasm and interest in a move into a PSL role. Ideally, they will need to be able to point to specific examples of PSL-related tasks they've undertaken alongside their fee-earning commitments.

Existing PSLs, too, are having to expand their skillset to keep pace with the developments in this area. Enthusiasm for knowledge sharing is essential, as is confidence in your own ability and being able to interact with those at all levels. To progress, PSLs now need to ensure that they have a full understanding of how they can add value and convince fee-earners, partners and the wider firm of the importance of knowledge sharing and the PSL function.

As ever, there is a need to be highly organised, but PSLs are now dealing with an increased number of competing deadlines. It's essential to deliver on a daily immediate basis whilst ensuring long-term strategic projects don't lose their momentum. The level of pressure has certainly increased, with one PSL we spoke to stating:

> *"It's always been a role where the ability to keep all plates spinning has been essential – but now there are more plates than ever!"*

How have the career structure and progression prospects evolved?

Progression opportunities and career paths for PSLs still vary considerably across the City. Some of the Magic Circle and larger firms now offer an "of counsel" position, which can be akin to partner level. A number of firms still have a flat structure where PSLs at all levels report into partners or group heads, and others offer a simple structure and reporting line as follows:

PSL – senior PSL/counsel – head of KM – global head of KM

However, as the role and its challenges have transformed, there is a growing demand from PSLs for their employers to provide a clear and defined career structure. Responses to this demand vary considerably at present, and whilst some firms have a lot of catching up to do, what is clear is that firms who are addressing this issue will find it easier to attract new talent and retain their existing PSL specialists. Management at one City firm recently commented:

> *"We are currently developing a career structure for our knowledge managers. They want a clear structure and motivating career prospects – just as our associates have a clear career path to guide and encourage them, so too should our PSLs. We want to encourage this talent and retain this valuable source of expertise."*

At an increasing number of firms, there are genuine opportunities to progress internally, or to be promoted into a lateral move as head of PSLs or head of knowledge management. For PSLs who find themselves in a career cul-de-sac, there are increasingly attractive alternatives elsewhere, providing they can embrace the new challenges and demands in this area.

In September 2018, it was reported in the legal press that one US firm had appointed a PSL as a partner. This is an extremely rare move, but a very encouraging one for those working in this area, as noted by *The*

Lawyer: "Few firms bring in PSLs at partner level, with the move representing a possible new career path for lawyers who have not followed the traditional track to partnership".[1]

In terms of remuneration, substantial bonuses are still the exception, but they do exist for high performers. Whilst salaries are certainly capped for standard PSL roles, financial rewards do exist where roles include a more strategic element. Firms are becoming increasingly aware that if they want to overhaul their PSL function, they will need to offer an attractive remuneration package. In the future, firms who genuinely buy into the PSL function and are prepared to invest in it will reap the rewards.

What does the international landscape look like?

In the US, the PSL role is a relatively new concept, and the market is this area is much less developed than in the UK. At the moment, these roles primarily exist in New York-based finance teams as KM attorneys.

In the Middle East it is a very small market; PSLs generally only exist at the larger international firms and often work in a more general KM capacity, with there being an expectation that PSLs will cover more than one area of speciality. The Asia & Pacific market is very similar, with only a small number of roles existing in Singapore, Hong Kong and Australia – again, with PSLs being expected to cover multiple practice areas. Commonly, a "transactional PSL" will provide support to the corporate and banking teams, and a "disputes PSL" will advise on arbitration, disputes and regulatory areas. Generally, the ratio of PSLs to fee-earners is much lower than in the UK.

So whilst internationally the role of the PSL isn't yet evolving as rapidly as it is in the UK, it is a developing trend and the level of investment in this area is likely to increase.

Conclusion

As we have seen, the nature and scope of the PSL role has evolved, which too has had a noticeable transformative effect on the demands made of the PSL and the challenges they face. A key element of the PSL role is now to promote and ensure collaboration across the firm, and PSLs need to encourage fee-earners, partners and other key teams in the firm to make a shared commitment to knowledge sharing and development. To progress, PSLs need to gain the respect and confidence of not just their practice group but of the wider firm, demonstrating that the role of the PSL is key to all of them.

However, whilst job titles and career structures still vary from firm to firm, the list of desirable characteristics for a PSL are consistent: Efficient.

Effective. Dynamic. Concise. Proactive. Adaptable. Innovative. Motivated. Forward thinking. Commercial acumen.

The role of a PSL is clearly more demanding than ever before, and this development is likely to continue. However, for those wishing to pursue a career in this area, the rewards are there. Transparent and progressive career structures are becoming more common, making the PSL route a challenging and interesting alternative to fee-earning. Exciting opportunities exist for those who embrace them.

Reference

1. Moloney, R. "From PSL to partner: Kirkland breaks new ground with Weil hire", *The Lawyer*, 5 September 2018. Available to access from: https://www.thelawyer.com/from-psl-to-partner-kirkland-breaks-new-ground-with-weil-hire/

Chapter 2: What should PSLs know? Creating your own KM competency framework

By Hélène Russell, founder of TheKnowledgeBusiness

"Professional support" lawyers (PSLs) have been around since the 1980s. Those in larger firms tend to have clear career paths, training programmes, and competency frameworks. Many smaller law firms, on the other hand, find that they have been gradually gaining knowledge lawyers for business reasons over the years, but have not yet developed appropriately tailored career paths or written competencies for them.

In smaller firms, the role of knowledge or support lawyer often develops ad hoc, with a job outline developed in isolation by the first PSL and then amended and passed on to the next incumbent; alternatively, a competency framework is created in-house for fee-earning lawyers and then adapted with no real understanding of knowledge management (KM) theory and practice, and how awareness of KM ought to permeate the role of the PSL.

Investing in creating or revamping competencies and a transparent career path for PSLs often gets kicked into the long grass as it is overtaken by easier and more urgent tasks; however, PSLs are a valuable and expensive resource, often with mixed utilisation, and deflected from achieving their highest potential return on investment.

To get the most value from their PSLs, law firms need to identify clear core competencies for them, encompassing their core legal field of expertise, business skills, people skills and also their skills in promoting learning and the management of knowledge within the teams they support.

This practical chapter looks at how a firm might develop those core competencies, drawing on confidential discussions with those who have developed frameworks recently and those who have had frameworks in place for many years, and advice from other similar sectors.

This chapter will explain the basics of competency frameworks but will focus primarily on the KM competencies which I believe should be included within the framework for your PSLs. It will set out competencies at various levels as examples, but you will need to complete your own research and modify these to suit the specific needs of your firm.

Competency frameworks: the basics

What are they and why are they needed?

A competency framework is a document that identifies the skills needed to perform a job within a particular organisation. Its main goal is to identify and communicate clearly the skills an employee needs to thrive in a job.

These frameworks are based on data gathered from those actually employed in certain roles, so they are useful in the recruitment process to accurately identify those candidates who already meet the role's needs. They also provide a clear framework for talent development and planning training, so that employees can improve the right skills and the areas of knowledge that the business needs from them, and performance and career development can be measured in a fair and transparent way. Lastly, having a competency model in place can also help management build a more diverse workforce by clarifying key factors such as cultural sensitivity, negotiation and facilitation, continuous learning, complex group dynamics, and by hiring based on independent data, rather than unconscious management bias.

A common issue, however, highlighted by The Chartered Institute of Personnel and Development (CIPD), is that competency frameworks will only be successful in supporting decision-making if they "accurately reflect the needs of both the job and the organisation in terms of skills, experience and behaviours". They should therefore take account of job and person specifications and the organisation's medium- and long-term needs for talent, as well as reflecting the organisational ethos and values.

Implemented well, competency frameworks are an opportunity for organisations to develop and sustain a competitive advantage in the market, hiring the right staff, developing existing staff, and ensuring roles are aligned to business goals.

Common examples

It is common for organisations to identify "core competencies" which are applicable to all employees – such as "customer focus", "teamworking" and "communication skills" – and "specific competencies", which apply to particular occupations.

There is no universally agreed best practice method for creating competency frameworks or for their content, so use this chapter and the additional reading at the end to inform the creation of your own tailored framework, designed to meet your particular organisation's needs. Do not, however, feel constrained by it.

Flexibility

Things change continuously. To reflect this – in particular, the changing nature of roles and career pathways as law firms adapt to technological advances – competency frameworks should be regularly reviewed and updated, taking into account the strategic needs of the future business in relation to its workforce and the likely nature and requirements of future roles.

Types of competency models

There are several types of competency models, which can be drawn together to meet your organisation's needs. Understanding these and how they align to your firm's vision and goals can help you decide which competency models to implement.

Organisational core competency model

Most organisations expect all employees to have a baseline set of skills that fit with its culture and vision for the future. These apply to all employees regardless of location or role, and they are crucial to the design, development or delivery of services to clients.

Core competencies must be able to be capable of being understood by all employees.

An organisational competency model enables you to understand and keep track of these essential core competencies and strive toward a workforce that has a balance of all those abilities.

For example, a firm-wide core competency might be that all members of your workforce must have foundational teamworking skills. This competency would specify what is expected – in terms of teamworking skills, knowledge sharing, and sharing tasks and success with others – and would give learning objectives in order to master that skillset.

Functional competency model

In addition to general, firm-wide competency expectations, functional competencies enable an employee to perform positively within a function or specific department. A few examples of functional competencies might be knowing certain computer programming languages, book-keeping skills, data analysis skills, etc.

Job competency model

The job competency model is similar to the functional competency model, but includes skillsets that are specifically needed for a certain role/job. This model focuses on clearly defined needs within a role in order to guarantee that each employee can perform to the best of their ability. The skillsets chosen when designing the competency framework are usually based on the skills of someone who is already performing well within that role and level.

Leadership competency model

When hiring for leadership roles, there are usually key essential competencies such as self-management and development, coaching and mentoring, and understanding and enforcing ethics, which can be incorporated into a specialist leadership competency model.

Each law firm is different, so I recommend that you combine and tailor the various models to create your own custom competency model, aligned to your organisation's vision, goals and strategy, to help everyone within the firm make aligned decisions to facilitate a swifter achievement of goals.

Creating your own PSL competencies framework

Although you can use outside consultants to develop the framework for your PSLs, you can also create your own competency framework in-house. It will require a significant investment of time, but you will hopefully create a more accurate framework – after all, who else understands your team and the skills needed for their roles better than those who work there?

If you plan to create your own framework, the following three principles are critical:

Involve the people doing the work

Competency frameworks should not be developed solely by HR staff or managers. They may be experts in their own fields, but they can't know what every role in the organisation involves. To understand what a role requires, you must talk to the person actually doing the job, their managers, peers, and perhaps even clients where a role is client-facing. In talking to them, you will understand what particular knowledge and skills make someone successful in that role.

Communicate

It is natural for people to worry about performance issues, change and strategic reviews. Designing a competency framework combines all of these, so make sure you clearly explain the process to everyone. Explain why you're developing the framework, how it will be created, how you'll use it and the benefits for the organisation as a whole and for them as individuals. The clearer your communication, the more relevant data you will receive, and the easier implementation will be.

Use relevant competencies only

Ensure that the competencies you include apply to all roles covered by the framework. If you include irrelevant competencies, people will lose faith in the framework in general. For example, if you created a single framework to cover the whole organisation, financial management would not then be included unless every worker had to demonstrate that skill. However, a framework covering only management roles would almost certainly involve competencies relating to financial management.

Competency framework creation process

This is the process involved in creating your own competency framework:

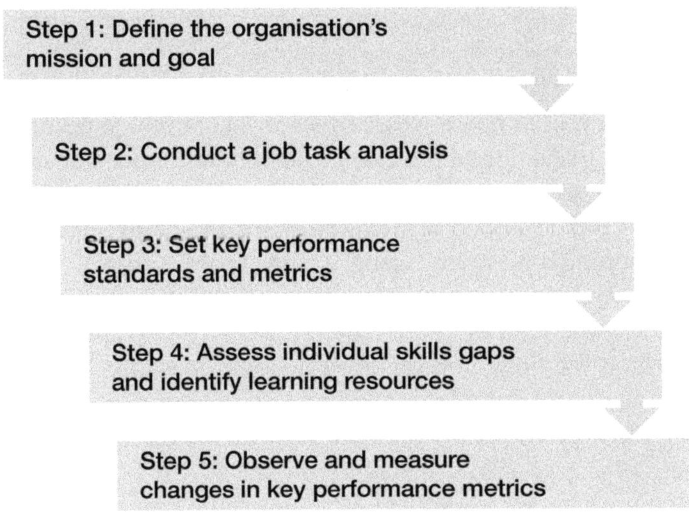

Figure 1: Competency framework creation process

The first and most critical step is for the organisation to identify its mission, goals and strategy, and ensure they are clearly defined. The organisation's strategy will be ineffective unless its employees' everyday actions support it.

I recommend that, at the end of your framework creation process, you revisit your firm's business goals and check again that the competencies contribute to the goals at the end of step two.

The second step is equally important. Each job role must be evaluated in-depth and the core competencies for success in that job role must be defined. This can be done using role-holder interviews and focus groups. You can also encourage employees to write diaries and blog posts to record their daily activities.

Ideally, all competencies for a job role should be identified and aligned with the organisation's mission and goals. Ask: "In what ways do PSLs add value to the business in this role?". Once that question is answered, review similar frameworks from other firms. Ensure that your framework is tailored to your organisation, rather than parachuted in from another firm, which will have different business needs and culture.

It is common to have four or five competencies and five levels of competency within each competency, but choose whatever levels suit your organisation best. It is common for levels one to three to focus on lower-order thinking skills (i.e. remembering, listing, finding, implementing, applying) and levels three to five to focus on higher-order thinking skills (i.e. designing, creating, experimenting, critiquing); however, again, ensure your levels suit your organisation rather than being constrained by this convention.

When determining the level of detail required within the competency definitions, consider these three important yet intangible factors:

- *The level to which behaviours in the skill definition are likely to vary together and in the same direction.* Often, proficiency in written and oral communications are combined into one skill. However, good speakers are not always good writers, and vice-versa;
- *The skills and definitions must be clearly understandable for the employees who will be subject to them.* The level of detail should be appropriate to the job, and using a level of language which they understand. Jargon should be used only where it acts as an appropriate short hand and common language; and
- *The use of observable, behavioural terms will ensure that the assessments are accurate and objective.* Descriptions written with objective terms should be created.

Lastly in this section, consult widely as to how PSLs benefit the organisation with a 360° analysis with all stakeholders, but sense-check responses with a small, trusted group who understand knowledge management.

Thirdly, appropriate performance standards must be established with workable metrics to measure them. This creates a baseline of the known minimum levels for the main job tasks. Where appropriate, the performance standards should include specific metrics such as minimum timings to complete certain tasks, or a minimum level of knowledge/ education/ training.

The fourth step in our framework creation process is more sensitive and evaluates each individual on their performance against the standards defined for their specific job role. Sufficiently detailed standards enable skills gaps to become apparent and should also identify learning resources and tools to close those gaps. Coaching is a useful tool to enable supervisors and employees to discuss closing the skills gaps. This is an often-neglected part of the process and requires proper resourcing and a clear implementation plan. Why identify gaps in performance if there is no plan to close them by upskilling your workforce?

Lastly, both individuals and the framework should be evaluated, monitored and measured over the long term. Where the competency framework remains relevant, this helps individuals to close their skills gaps and enables organisations to avoid the common problem highlighted by the CIPD, ensuring the framework remains relevant to the organisation as it is and for the future. You might also want to devise suitable questions to include within your group reflective practices (such as After Action Reviews) and client reviews, connected to your competency framework, to ensure that it is reviewed and kept up-to-date automatically during other business processes.

Hopefully you now have a clearer idea what competency frameworks are, what value they offer, and the process for creating them. I now consider what aspects of KM skills and knowledge ought to be part of the technical skills expected within a PSL competency framework.

Firstly, should we expect PSLs to be measured against KM competencies at all? Many are untrained in KM. My own view is that where a firm is large enough to have separate KMers, PSLs can act as subject matter experts and leave the KM skills to others, but in smaller firms PSLs will have to take on the KM roles and become dual experts both in their legal subject matter and also in the best ways to deliver learning and knowledge sharing.

To create a detailed and comprehensive framework of competencies of your own for those who work in knowledge management, I recommend that you read the PhD of Dr Andre Saito "Educating Knowledge Managers: a competence-based approach" from September 2007.[1] You could either adopt his various headings for competencies or design your own.

I recommend that you study the Knowledge Cycle for KM activities (see

Figure 2 below) and, to inform the different levels within each competency category, consider the APQC KM maturity model[2] and lower/higher thinking orders. Dixon's "Three Eras of KM"[3] is useful for both activities and levels.

I recommend these models because they are the simplest and most relevant (to legal KM), and they ought to readily adapt to the different needs of legal firms, which can be highly individualistic in their requirements of PSLs.

The Knowledge Cycle breaks KM activities down into the following:

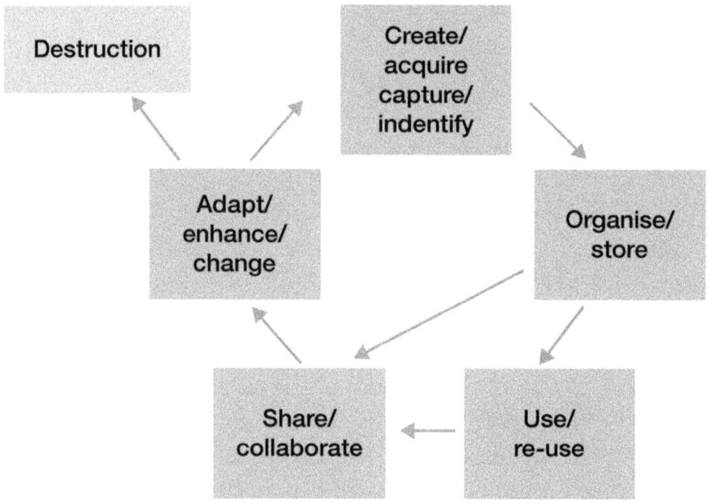

Figure 2: The Knowledge Cycle

You could use the knowledge cycle as the basis for your categories of competencies, e.g.:

1. Knowledge creation, learning and reflection;
2. Knowledge storage, management and reuse;
3. Knowledge sharing and collaborating; and
4. Adapting, enhancing and changing knowledge.

Alternatively, you could focus on the type of knowledge being managed and use:

1. Management of explicit knowledge;
2. Management of tacit and implicit knowledge;

3. Management of process;
4. Management of expertise and relationships; and
5. Management of culture and organisational change.

In this example, client knowledge and consideration of the Knowledge Cycle would be included within each category.

For the different levels within each competency, I would refer to the APQC maturity model:

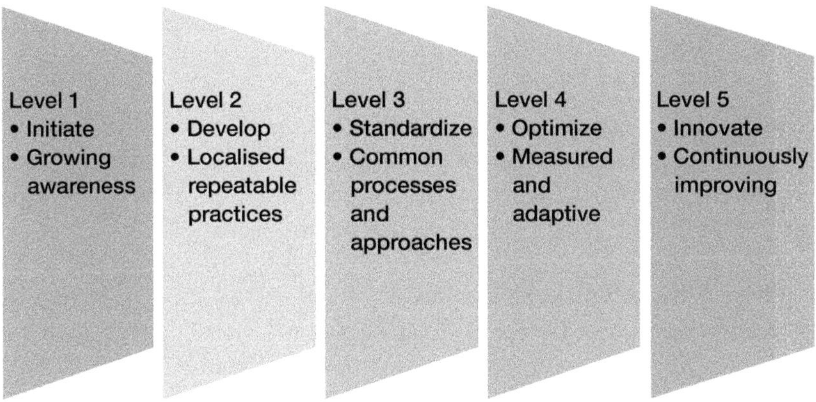

Figure 3: The APC maturity model[4]

For both activities and levels you could use Nancy Dixon's "Three Eras of KM" as a reference, which divides KM activities into:

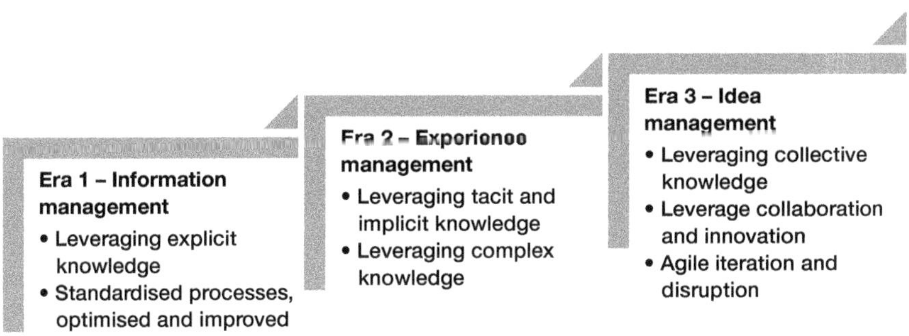

Figure 4: Three Eras of KM[5]

Law firms would usually undertake knowledge work within all three Eras: optimising precedents, practice notes and databases of explicit knowledge; creating supervision, shadowing and peer assist programmes; workshops and encouraging working out loud (WOL) and agile programmes.

There will be activities and competencies at all levels from each Era in your framework, but my own experience is that activities within Eras 2 and 3 are generally more complex to implement, so might feature more in the higher levels within your framework.

Example PSL KM framework

I have included these competencies as an example of what you could create for your firm. There is no best practice example for KM competencies for PSLs and I do not claim these are a gold-standard or benchmark. The competencies you create will depend on the needs of your firm and the department or team the PSL supports. Hopefully, however, these will assist you in creating your own tailored competencies.

1 Management of learning, capture and creation of knowledge

Blending the APQC maturity model, Dixon's Three Eras model and lower/higher orders of thinking, levels for learning could – depending on current and future business needs – look something like this:

> *"Level 1 – Can identify the different modes of teaching adults. Can explain Kolb's learning cycle and supports fee earners in relation to their reflective learning. Implements learning strategies created by in-house learning and development specialists. Delivers current awareness as required by team in consultation with in-house information and learning experts. Identifies gaps in knowledge and consults with internal learning and development specialists for support/advice."*

The highest level could look something like this:

> *"Level 5 – Keeps up-to-date on latest research into adult learning/andragogy and analyses new trends for strengths and weaknesses and develops his/her practice accordingly, piloting and experimenting with new projects to improve learning outcomes. Promotes/advocates for a learning organisation. Anticipates and identifies future strategic business learning needs and creates appropriate programmes to fill gaps, developing business cases where investment is required. Measures learning outcomes appropriately and adapts programmes to maximise learning effectiveness within budget."*

Levels 2–4 would be adjusted to suit your firm's needs between these two parameters.

2 Management of storing, organising, use and re-use of knowledge

Again, depending on your firm's strategic needs, your Level 1 competency for the skills involved in management of storing, organising, use and re-use of knowledge could be:

> *"Level 1 – Can explain the knowledge cycle and identify different types of knowledge (tacit, implicit and explicit). Can explain how management differs for each type of knowledge. Maintains a system for the storage, organisation, use and re-use of knowledge. Assists with creation of checPSLists for improved processes. Assists with knowledge audits and implements information and knowledge policies. Implements business strategy in relation to organisation of knowledge artefacts and is familiar with all IT systems used. Brings gaps in service which are identified by service users to the attention of the appropriate expert."*

> *"Level 5 – Can explain Nonaka's SECI model, analyse it and identify strengths and weaknesses as they apply within the organisation. Is an advocate for knowledge sharing. Designs and builds systems for content management (knowledge repositories, portals, online libraries) or takes a leadership role in assessing the needs of the organisation and analysing how proposed technologies meet those needs. Can create a knowledge management and storage strategy for his/her department. Can create measurements for individual KM projects and understand how to avoid the gaming of measurements. Understands and acts upon the limitations of codification of knowledge. Understands the benefits of and uses gamification. Designs programmes on strategic needs of the business. Identifies gaps in knowledge sharing and, based on future strategic needs of the business, creates business plans to head off future problems. Is a vocal advocate for knowledge sharing for business purposes. Adapts to changing needs and remains agile and flexible."*

Again, Levels 2–4 would be adjusted to suit the business's needs between these two boundaries. I would suggest that Level 3 contains competencies about mapping knowledge, taxonomies and the identification and discussion of risks associated with new solutions to knowledge storage and management problems.

3 Knowledge sharing and collaborating

> *"Level 1 – Can explain the importance of knowledge sharing and the value of person-to-person knowledge transfer and facilitates this as directed. Uses*

storytelling as appropriate. Works to improve his/her network. Supports the organisation in overcoming common barriers to knowledge sharing. Promotes creativity and innovation. Can identify internal experts in different fields within an existing expert system and connect employees to the right expert."

"Level 5 – Can explain Snowden's heuristics. Can design, explain and direct implementation of knowledge sharing systems based on the strategic needs of the organisation. Can identify and support communities of practice where they emerge. Can analyse social networks, highlight gaps and risks to the business as a result and develop strategic programmes to mitigate those risks. Can explain the value of and lead Gurteen Knowledge Cafes. Creates stimulating work systems which encourage knowledge sharing, curiosity, creativity and collaboration. Can explain the work of Gardner and develops strategic plans to implement Smart Collaboration where appropriate to business needs. Forecasts strategic knowledge sharing needs and develops appropriate systems to meet those needs. Advocates for others to receive professional development to assist them in developing innovative solutions. Engages with thought leaders in the field. Analyses new knowledge sharing trends for strengths and weaknesses and acts accordingly. Identifies and develops opportunities to collaborate widely with internal and external stakeholders."

Again, between these two margins, you can design appropriate levels. I would suggest that an appropriate Level 3 would include, amongst others: *"Explores new ways to solve problems and engage colleagues from different areas within the organisation. Actively engages in knowledge sharing and promotes it to others. Seeks out opportunities to share their knowledge."*

4 Adapt, enhance, change knowledge

"Level 1 – Awareness of basic root cause analysis, quality assurance and post action reflection tools. Is adaptable and supports change."

"Level 5 – High level of understanding and application of quality assurance, process management and automation. Knowledgeable of systems thinking, design thinking and complex systems. Promotes a 'safe-to-fail' or 'fail fast' environment, encouraging new ideas and experimentation in knowledge delivery solutions. Embraces change proactively. Creates change management programmes using current best practice. Thinks strategically about present and future risks during changes. Has a basic knowledge of complexity and Cynefin Sense-Making."

In between these levels, I would expect Level 3 to include something about the ability to analyse and map processes and identify process improvements, but perhaps not necessarily an understanding of Six Sigma, Kaizen and Lean, etc.

Conclusion

Competency frameworks benefit organisations by improving hiring and performance management, building a workforce with the right skills to deliver its strategic goals.

Where PSLs work without specialist KM support in law firms, I recommend that their competency framework includes competencies relating to knowledge management skills, in order to ensure that their activities are the most efficient and effective ways to deliver the knowledge needs of their teams. This chapter has suggested some examples of KM competencies which PSLs could be expected to adopt, but it is important that, when these frameworks are designed, they are tailored to your firm's specific needs to support the delivery of your firm's goals.

Lastly, remember that competence in general is related to action. It involves the mobilisation of resources to meet external demands. Whatever competencies you decide are most important for your PSLs within your organisation, you must ensure that your staff are exposed to new situations and challenges to ensure that they grow through experiential learning and reflection.

References

1. A. Saito (2007) "Educating Knowledge Managers: A Competence-based approach" https://dspace.jaist.ac.jp/dspace/bitstream/10119/3739/2/121paper.pdf (accessed Sept 2018). For further reading, please see A. Saito (2016), "Modelling individual KM competencies", Real KM blog https://realkm.com/2016/04/13/modelling-individual-km-competencies-ekm-series/ (accessed Sep 2018)
2. APQC's white paper on using their KM maturity model is available to download here for free https://www.apqc.org/knowledge-base/documents/using-apqcs-levels-knowledge-management-maturity (accessed Sept 2018)
3. Dixon, N. M. (2018) "The three eras of knowledge management" in J. P. Girard & J.L. Girard (Eds) "Knowledge management matters: Words of wisdom from leding practitioners" (19-47). Macon, GA: Sagology
4. Dixon, N. M. (2012) "The three Eras of Knowledge Management" http://www.nancydixonblog.com/2012/08/the-three-eras-of-knowledge-management.html (accessed Sept 2018)
5. APQC (2017) "How mature is your KM program?" https://www.apqc.org/knowledge-base/download/250280/K03302_How%20Mature%20is%20

Your%20KM%20Program%20Updated%20March%202017.pdf (accessed Sept 2018)

6. This is my own adaptation of Nancy Dixon's diagram from her "Three Eras" blog posts and video.

Chapter 3: Demonstrating the value of professional support

By Catherine Hart, partner and PSL at Digby Brown

A perennial issue for PSLs is the question of how we demonstrate the value of the work that we undertake. This is something unique to PSLs as solicitors because – unlike the majority of colleagues in private practice – we do not earn fees and therefore do not generate income for the business in a readily demonstrable way.

In this chapter, we will consider why it is important that PSLs are able to demonstrate the value that they provide and look at some practical ways that can help those working in professional support to do so.

Why is it important that PSLs are able to demonstrate value?

I have little doubt that any team or department which benefits from the support of an effective PSL will be fully aware of the value that PSLs can add, and probably regard their PSL as essential to the team's success. The challenge for PSLs, however, is how to demonstrate that value in a wider business context. Professional support can sometimes be seen as an optional extra – a "nice-to-have" – rather than an essential. As PSLs do not generate income through fees, they tend to be regarded as a cost and, on that basis, it is important that PSLs are able to demonstrate the value they bring.

I would suggest that finding an empirical method of demonstrating the value of professional support work, in a similar way to those used to measure the performance of a fee-earner or department, will always be a challenge. A PSL may spend hours putting together and delivering a programme of training sessions which better equip the fee-earners to meet their clients' needs, but it is unlikely that the value of the training delivered will be measurable in a way that will have a demonstrable effect on the team's profitability.

In a sector where generating fees equates to delivering value, PSLs have to be creative in finding ways to demonstrate the value they can bring.

To time-record or not?

When the role first developed, some would argue that one of the advantages was the pressure to record time in units and to account in this way for the work undertaken each day was removed, as PSLs were not usually expected to time-record. Indeed, the time recording systems used by many practices did not readily lend themselves to use by non-fee-earners, due to the categories under which time could be recorded.

This has changed over time, however, and many legal businesses now expect PSLs to time-record and have separate time-recording categories that reflect the various aspects of the role. Having said that, there are still a good number of legal practices that are content for their PSLs not do so.

I have mixed views about the benefits of time-recording from a PSL's perspective. Fundamentally, the role developed to allow professional support tasks to be undertaken by lawyers who were not subject to the pressure to generate fees and were therefore free to devote the time required to other tasks. It could be argued that, by encouraging PSLs to time record, businesses are introducing an element of pressure that can hinder the effective use of the PSL's time. In my experience, as soon as you have to account for the time spent on a task or project in this way, an element of pressure is introduced.

The most effective PSLs have strong time-management skills and are able to assess how much time is required for a particular task. PSLS frequently must juggle a number of completing calls on their time, and they do not necessarily need to time-record to prioritise tasks efficiently.

On the other hand, by recording time, particularly if a task is related to a specific client matter – for example, a complex piece of research or a detailed note the interpretation of legislative provisions – there is a clear record of the time that a PSL has spent on a task which, had it not been for the PSL's involvement, a fee-earner might well have had to undertake. If the client is charged for this work, its value will be quantifiable. The time spent on client matters can be added up over the course of a year and used to reflect the value of the PSL's input to the work of a team or department.

However, if the task is not related to a client matter, it could be argued that recording the time spent on that task is less of a measure of the PSL's value. For example, a PSL might spend a great deal of time drafting and revising precedents, but if the fee-earners do not use these the time spent on this task is not adding value – in the same way as a fee-earner may spend hours on a piece of work, but the client ultimately cannot be charged for this and so the time is eventually written off.

Nevertheless, there are those who find it beneficial to record the time that has been spent on various tasks, if for no other reason than providing visibility of the various areas in which the PSL has provided input as well as the breadth of these. In a sense, this demonstrates the value of the role. This record can also be referred to in response to the occasionally asked question: "What does the PSL do?"

In addition, if much of the PSL's time is spent supporting a small number of fee-earners on individual tasks, this sometimes leads to the situation where others are not aware of exactly what tasks or projects the PSL has been involved in. Recording time can assist in providing a useful picture of the extent of professional support provided.

Freeing up fee-earner time

The whole point of the professional support role is to enable fee-earners to work more effectively and efficiently; as the pressure on fee-earners to generate profit increases, the need for effective professional support is even greater.

In many legal practices, the more traditional PSL tasks – for example, developing and maintaining precedents, writing legal updates and delivering training – are all still seen as valuable ways of providing that support. However, with the development of external online resources, such as precedents and practice notes and tailored current awareness solutions, PSLs are finding that they have more time to focus on other, perhaps less traditional, areas.

Many PSLs undertake alternative tasks that fee-earners might otherwise have to do – for example, writing website content, contributing to tender documents and pitches, and preparing presentations. With at least some of these tasks, the time involved is quantifiable. If a PSL therefore writes an article or the script for a presentation, the time spent is time that a fee-earner doesn't have to sacrifice. Even if there is not a formal time-recording system in place, it is worth keeping a record of the time spent on such tasks over the course of a year so that this information can be used to demonstrate the saving in fee-earners' time. Because many PSLs are highly experienced, they are often asked to undertake tasks that would otherwise fall to partners or senior associates, whose time has a high value.

PSLs have frequently come to the role with a background in fee-earning, so understand the work that the fee-earners are undertaking and the pressures they face. This means that they are well-placed to identify processes that could be more efficient and to work on solutions for their improvement. PSLs are often instrumental in helping to ensure consistency of practice and improving standards. Savings in time can be made by implementing tools that avoid the need to "reinvent the wheel", such as standard documentation, checklists and guidance notes.

The challenge is to demonstrate the return on these initiatives, because this will invariably be difficult to quantify, and to measure the savings in time achieved. Although it would be challenging to do this in a particularly precise way, it can be worth working out on a rough basis how much fee-earner time is saved on an individual basis. Multiplied by the number of fee-earners in a team or department over the course of a year, this can provide at least an indication of the time that the innovation or initiative has freed up.

Ultimately, however, the value may be demonstrated by the fact that the fee-earners are able to focus on their cases or transactions, working cost effectively, consistently and to a high standard.

Demonstrating value through savings

It will be clear by now that demonstrating the value of the PSL role is a challenge, and we often have to think creatively about ways to do this.

One that I have encountered, but which might not be immediately obvious, is finding ways to make savings for the business. This approach is probably best explained with a couple of practical examples.

A PSL joined a large department that had no formal CPD programme and routinely sent more junior fee-earners to external courses, at significant cost to the business. She recognised that there was a great deal of knowledge and experience within the department that was not being shared. Indeed, many of the areas covered by the external sessions could have been dealt with just as effectively by tapping into the in-house talent. The PSL set up an internal CPD programme with regular sessions and an annual training day, which together covered most of the fee-earners' CPD requirements. She also took over responsibility for authorising and booking places at external events. This allowed the PSL to monitor requests and develop the internal programme to meet the needs of the fee-earners so that, in time, only those needing information that could not be delivered effectively in-house were allowed to attend external events. Over the course a year, the PSL was able to point to a demonstrable saving in the department's training budget.

The business was so impressed that this model was subsequently rolled out across other departments, leading to further savings.

In another practice, an electronic document sharing facility had been introduced, but there was internal and external resistance to using this. Recognising this, the PSL worked with those who had set up the new facility to deliver training to both the fee-earners and external recipients on the use and benefits of the process. He also developed guidance on the appropriate use of this facility and, as a result of these measures, the use of the online document sharing facility increased significantly, with resultant measurable savings in the copying and postage costs incurred by the business. Although not directly responsible for the introduction of the facility, the PSL was able to use his experience to identify both why there was reluctance to use this and how this would be best addressed.

PSLs as the centre of the business

One of the key benefits of the professional support role that I am always keen to promote is the ability to provide a connection between fee-earners and other areas of the business. I would suggest that PSLs have a unique vantage point – not only do they understand what is required of fee-earners, but it is likely that their role will bring them into contact with other areas of the business, such as IT and business development. This allows PSLs to develop a relationship with colleagues who work in those areas and to cultivate a collaborative approach. PSLs can develop an understanding of how other parts of the business operate and the projects that are proposed or underway, which in turn may open up the opportunity to feed into those projects. This also allows the PSL to become involved in the early stages of any business development, when there is more opportunity to influence the process with a view to minimising the disruption and maximising the benefits to fee-earners.

I know of several PSLs who have played an integral part in large business-wide projects precisely because of the unique position they hold. One example might be the introduction of a new case management system, which combines an understanding of how the fee-earners work, operational aspects of the business, and the technology required.

PSLs also often have the vision to take ideas and processes utilised elsewhere in the business and suggest ways in which these might be adapted for use in other areas, which increases the value of such processes and can lead to savings for the business.

This is part of the value of the role that should not be overlooked or underestimated. PSLs are uniquely placed to see the bigger picture and are not afraid to embrace change in an effort to drive up standards and increase efficiency.

Don't be afraid to step up!

PSLs have often developed many different skills that can be put to good use in the wider business context. I would encourage PSLs to look for areas to become involved in that may not necessarily be part of traditional professional support role, but where the knowledge and experience of a

PSL can be well-utilised. PSLs are also often in a position to devote more time to large-scale projects because they are not subject to the pressure to generate fees. As an example, I have had an interest in risk management for a number of years; when I recognised the opportunity for a centralised risk management role, this was something I was keen to take on. This has involved drafting and developing policies and overseeing compliance across the business.

Project management is another area to which the skillset of PSLs is well-suited. Strong project managers are highly organised and good at prioritising tasks, as well as being effective communicators who have sound problem-solving and people skills. These are all attributes required to be an effective PSL.

Develop and implement a business plan

There will be many PSLs who already produce an annual business plan in relation to the professional support provided, or perhaps feed into a departmental plan.

Others, however, will not have undertaken this exercise, but I would suggest that it is definitely worth considering, as a well-considered plan can be a very useful way of demonstrating value to the wider business.

This need not be a complex or highly detailed strategy, but should be used to set out the focus of professional support over the next twelve months. It is vital that the professional support plan ties in with the strategy of the team or department that the PSL works with. For example, is the department planning to develop into an area of practice that has not previously been a focus? Recognising this, the professional support plan could set out some practical steps that the PSL will undertake to support this objective – for example, develop a bank of precedents, source training, or introduce a method of sharing knowledge readily. Is the team or department planning to target a new source of business? The professional support plan could set out some steps to assist, such as writing a series of articles showcasing the team's knowledge in this area or planning and developing training sessions that could be offered to potential clients.

If a business plan is to be used effectively to demonstrate the value of the PSL role, the focus should be on tangible outcomes so that, looking back on the year, the PSL can confirm which outcomes have been met and, if possible, the effects of these. Be realistic – if your plan is overambitious, you are likely to lose credibility. It is also important to make sure that the outcomes in your business plan are measurable so that progress can be assessed.

A business plan also helps to give the PSL visibility in the business generally and to reinforce the message that professional support has an important part to play in the same way as other areas of the business.

If you do not already produce a business plan, why not suggest this and explain the benefits? Although this will add a task to your undoubtedly already long list, it is likely to be worthwhile in helping to demonstrate the value of the professional support provided.

The power of feedback

One of the most helpful ways I have found to demonstrate my value is through obtaining feedback. Legal directories often include feedback quotes from colleagues and satisfied clients in relation to featured solicitors, and there is no reason why PSLs should not use feedback from colleagues to demonstrate their value.

As well as the routine feedback received from colleagues in response to specific assistance they have had, I actively seek feedback on various aspects of professional support through online surveys, which the teams I support are asked to complete. Provided completing these is not too onerous and the requests for feedback are not too frequent, my experience is that fee-earners are quite happy to provide their comments. Questions can be tailored to ensure feedback demonstrates the value that professional support provides – for example, "How many times a week/month do you use the following resources?" or "How would you rate the usefulness of the team's knowledgebank?"

Not only is the feedback collected useful in demonstrating the value of the support provided to those who benefit directly from this, it also helps to identify what is working well and any areas needing further improvement.

The online knowledgebank my team has developed can generate reports that detail the number of times that areas of the knowledgebank are accessed; statistics such as these can also help to demonstrate the value of a well-used resource.

Conclusion

It has to be accepted that the work produced in the PSL role often does not lend itself readily to being valued in a similar way to that of fee-earners. As a result, PSLs have to be inventive in finding ways to demonstrate their value, not only in relation to the tasks they already undertake, but also in seeking other areas in which their wide skillset and experience can add value.

The vast majority of PSLs are motivated by the desire to make the job of the fee-earners easier and to help them work more efficiently. They are aware of the pressure that fee-earners face and actively looking for ways to support them. If we achieve this, that, in essence, is the value we provide.

It could be argued that if PSLs focus too heavily on being able to quantify the value they bring, this might undermine their effectiveness. However, it is important to the development of the role that PSLs are able to demonstrate value. Hopefully this chapter has provided some ideas on practical ways to do so, both in financial terms and more generally.

Chapter 4:

Adding value for clients and the team – optimising the use of client-facing knowledge products

By Katherine Lang, senior PSL at Taylor Wessing

A client relationship builder, a leader and an innovator! Ten years ago, these were all attributes PSLs were predicted to require in the future. Juliet Humphries, in her book *The Changing Role of the Professional Support Lawyer* (2008), envisaged the emergence of the "third-generation" PSL, who would be key in building the firm's client relationships and a leader in establishing new ways of meeting clients' needs.

In this chapter, I examine just how much the role of the PSL has evolved into this sophisticated "third generation role".

As examined by Julia Bateman in chapter 10 of this book, we can assume that a PSL has built a large body of specialist expertise through the following:

- Awareness of legislative priorities in their practice area;
- Knowledge of recent developments in case law;
- Examination of key consultations; and
- Examination of relevant government reports.

The next step is to ask. how can a "third-generation" PSL best leverage this extensive body of knowledge to generate value for clients and the firm?

It is clear that this will vary from firm to firm, and even between teams within a firm. However, in my experience, this can be done through the efficient use of generic and tailored knowledge products, the optimisation of those products for the relevant audience, and by a critical examination of the value of online content. This chapter will examine each of these areas in turn, starting with the key question…

How can PSLs use knowledge more efficiently?

Third-generation PSLs should be able to employ their specialist expertise and content efficiently – a piece of insight should be able to be utilised several times with equal impact.

As Susskind notes in *Tomorrow's Lawyers* (2017), "regarding legal work as bespoke in nature is an unhelpful – if often romantic – fiction ... I contend that deploying bespoke techniques in many instances is to adopt cottage-industry methods when mass production and mass customization techniques are now available to support the delivery of a less costly yet better service".

The life-cycle of knowledge

In my view, the best way to view the life-cycle of a piece of knowledge or content is through the following flow diagram:

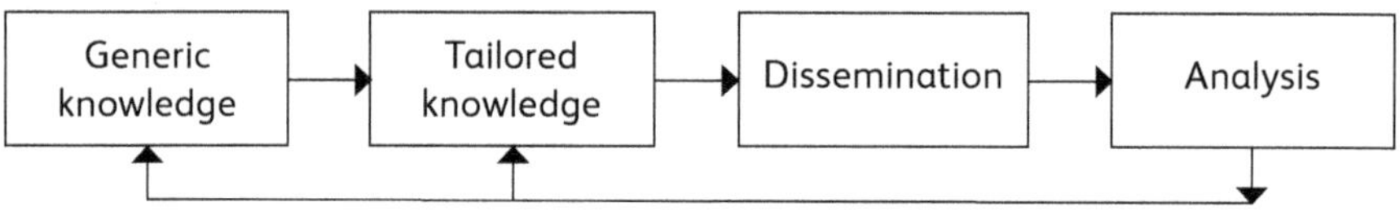

Figure 1: The life-cycle of knowledge

I will now examine each element of this diagram in turn.

Generic knowledge

A piece of generic knowledge is something that is aimed at all clients or target clients, perhaps narrowed to a specific grouping or sector, but available for wide dissemination.

This could include articles in external publications, external podcasts or videos, and departmental or sector newsletters.

Tailored knowledge

Tailored or bespoke knowledge, on the other hand, is designed with a more defined audience in mind. It is intended to be used to maintain existing relationships, add value for existing clients, or to be used as a "value-add" product as a marketing tool.

Of course, this tailored knowledge does not have to be new content, generated separately from the generic knowledge referred to above. It can be based on the generic knowledge, but refined in order to create items such as brochures ("Key sector trends in..."), client newsletters ("Horizon-scanning in..."), or video content or "listicles" for the millennial audience.

...feeds into client training

All of the above can be fed into a generic base client "training menu", which sets out pre-prepared sessions that can be led either by the relevant PSL or an experienced member of the team. The knowledge is already within the team; it just needs to be re-purposed. It can also be readily tailored for specific clients.

How can PSLs optimise content for maximum engagement?

When creating a generic or tailored generic piece for consumption by a current or prospective client, the key question is how to ensure that it is read. Time-pressed lawyers can be tempted to take an interesting piece of information generated as part of a real-life matter, anonymise it and add an enticing title, assuming that this will be a worthwhile piece of material to post online as a client bulletin.

However, different rules apply to articles and bulletins than to notes containing legal advice, and much has been written by academic experts on the science of user experience and engagement. This is not straightforward – but it is part of the skill-set of the third-generation PSL, who will be adept at tailoring content for a digital environment.

So how can you optimise a newsletter for a readership that will most likely read that newsletter in a hurry on their smart phone? How do you entice them to click on your newsletter in an inbox that is already bursting at the seams?

Whether a PSL is writing or editing content, they should be considering the following points:

The inverted pyramid: need-to-know vs nice-to-have

A useful guide for reader-friendly content is to use the inverted pyramid – a journalistic tool whereby the most important information (the "need-to-know") is presented first, followed by further background and details (the "nice-to-have"). This is ideal when writing online content – even those who skim, or quickly click off the page, should take away the key point.

Consumption of the information cake

It is now well-known that web content is often scanned by readers in an F-shape. Other scanning patterns have also been identified, such as the "layer-cake" pattern where the eyes scan headings and sub-headings only, and the "spotted" pattern, where readers scan the text for specific items such as embedded links.[1, 2] This is problematic when content has been carefully crafted but readers only engage with part of it.

This can be addressed, at least in part, by good design and writing practice. It is clear that, in many cases, the first few lines of text are consumed by more readers than subsequent text on the same page, and that the first few words on the left of each line of text are viewed for longer than those on the right. So, make the most important points early in the piece.

Subheadings, bullet points, and "information scent"

It is positive that lawyers naturally gravitate towards creating text containing subheadings and bullet-pointed lists, as we are trained from an early stage that this is how clients like to read our advice. The use of pertinent and interesting sub-headings and bulleted lists in online content can generate better reader engagement – at Taylor Wessing we like to use sub-headings framed as intriguing questions, providing "information scent" which draws the reader into the text below.

Accessibility: not all readers are the same

Readers can also be drawn to focus on relevant text by the use of bold font for important words and phrases, and by grouping small amounts of important content in a box or with a coloured background. It is best to ensure that embedded links include information-bearing words if you want to encourage readers to click through to information elsewhere on your website – this also improves accessibility for blind or partially-sighted readers who hear links read aloud (rather than "read more", a link could instead be formatted to say "explore further information on changes to the Land Registration Act 2002"). The obvious point is to ensure that newsletters are correctly formatted for reading on a smartphone screen.

Lawyers need to be trained to create content that is readable online, a skill which differs greatly from drafting a legal document. At Taylor Wessing we run writing workshops specifically for this purpose, where the facilitator will critique pieces of writing previously published by the course delegates.

Dissemination of online content

Once you have generated tailored, up-to-date and insightful content, how do you share it with the wider world?

Looking back almost 30 years ago, publications for law firms on winning and retaining new clients did not envisage any engagement beyond hard copy brochures. For example, Edward Wright's *How to win new clients and keep them* (1991) devotes a chapter to printing and suggests that clients may appreciate newsletters and booklets on selected key topics. Some advice is sound to this day – for example, the recommendation to keep articles short so that they arouse interest and persuade people to contact you for further information.

However the expectation of frequency of contact has perhaps changed: the advice is to give yourself a little flexibility by avoiding a definite monthly or quarterly commitment. Of course, the immediacy of contact was not envisaged in the early 1990s: the reader is advised to ensure that the brochure's reply instructions are clear and inviting, and readers are warned that most brochures need to incorporate a reply device such as a tear-off coupon.

Nowadays, it is tempting to assume that it is sufficient to generate a pertinent piece of knowledge and then simply to drop it online. But this is not enough. A team needs to use this knowledge to actively engage with clients. As Susskind notes, "clients respond favourably, for example, to law firms that express ongoing, and even passionate, interest in them… they appreciate periodic briefings on the trends and developments that may have a direct impact on them. Maintaining this sort of rolling contact does not come naturally to many lawyers and is often trumped by chargeable work for other clients. This is regrettable because this kind of regular interaction is increasingly vital for the long-term relationships that clients are now deeming important."

This is where the third-generation PSL comes in. Of course, rolling client contact can be overshadowed by a pressing deadline for an ongoing deal. However, if a PSL has engaged with the business plan of the team and those clients that have been identified as priorities or key targets, the goal of regular and targeted contact can be achieved.

Personal emails

A PSL can work directly with the business development team to assess which clients are top of the priority list, and examine what might be concerning them. If a generic piece has been created, as noted above, it does not take long to tailor this to a particular client, and then ask the client relationship partner to send this to their main contact in a friendly email.

Dedicated online landing page and client microsites

Look at how content is shared on social media. Does your firm have a dedicated landing page on its website for online content, with links to the relevant authors' biographies? Put new content here, even if it has been written for an external publication. This means that when articles are shared on social media, readers who click through to the article are immediately drawn into the firm's website rather than straight to the website of the publication. Even if the publication embargoes its content, the firm will usually be permitted to post an embedded link on its website, with biographies and a short summery of the piece. You are then in control of analysing views and click-throughs related to this piece. Often publications will also share their own analytics of a piece with the authors, if requested.

Clients often have greater appetite for a cross-practice area approach. If, for example, a client is an overseas entity investing in UK property, they may be interested in such diverse areas as the firm's corporate finance, tax, banking and real estate practices. They will not want to click across the landing pages for each of these practice areas. It is better to have a microsite for this type of client, on which updates across each of these practice areas are posted. Taylor Wessing has microsites, such as Synapse, which provides regular updates on law for life sciences. This is an unrestricted microsite which is available through the firm's website.

An additional value-added tool, for key clients, is the client extranet. This is a web-based portal with restricted access, which delivers specific legal updates and other knowledge products such as precedents tailored specifically for that client. PSLs across various practice areas will be responsible for including content relevant to that client. The client benefits by having access to up-to-date knowledge, specially selected for them, all in one place. The firm benefits by ensuring that its name and branding are associated with a one-stop-shop for the client's in-house legal team. This can be a resource-intensive product for a firm to offer, but one which can reap rewards when used selectively.

Client newsletter/mailing lists

However, don't exclusively share content on social media. Lawyers can often be wary of bombarding their clients with emails, and perhaps overly pessimistic in assuming that competitors are already generating identical content. But whilst it is no longer the paper newsletter described by Wright in 1991, received in the morning's post or handed out to prospective clients with its tear-off contact slip, there is still an important place for the client newsletter.

As highlighted by Nielsen, "email newsletters are a better way to stay in touch with customers than updates posted on social networks … a newsletter goes into the inbox and sits there, whereas social networks use a stream-based interface metaphor, where new postings constantly replace old ones… your newsletter subscribers are usually your most loyal customers and fans, so it's important to treat them better than the more fickle audience on social networks".[3] Given that a newsletter has greater longevity, it makes sense to take time in crafting its content.

Decision engines – the interactive tear-off contact slip?

A new, complex piece of legislation can provide fertile ground for the use of online content to engage with current and prospective clients.

As well as sharing updates through personal emails, social media, online landing pages and client newsletters, recent innovations in AI and IT now enable firms to produce interactive web applications. These can be used to inform clients of new legislation, conduct an initial analysis of how it will affect them, and suggest the level of support that they require.

Taylor Wessing has developed its TW:navigate product, which is an online tool that has now been used in relation to several pieces of legislation, including the PSC or "Persons with Significant Control" register, the Modern Slavery Act 2015, the Criminal Finances Act 2017 and EEA personal data transfer. Through the Taylor Wessing website, users are invited to input details into the free, confidential online diagnostic tool. This information is then assessed in order to offer the client or prospective client an initial view on how the legislation will affect them, and suggest the level of support that they may require.

This is a new generation of knowledge product. Traditionally, a paper-based questionnaire would have been used to assist clients in assessing what category they fell into, but this runs the risk of being too time-consuming and expensive. TW:navigate serves two purposes: it acts as a "triage", helping clients to assess the level of legal advice that they need; it is also, however, an "interactive tear-off contact slip" in that it enables the firm to harvest data on who is using the tool.

Taylor Wessing won the "Innovation in Knowledge Management Award" at The Lawyer's Business Leadership Awards 2016 for TW:navigate. It is a good example of the third-generation PSL with expert knowledge of the legislation working together with a member of the firm's Innovation Hub, adept at mobilising technology for legal services, and a member of the relevant fee earning team.

How do we assess the value of content generated and placed online?

Engaging with your content, once it is out in the big wide digital world

There is no point in generating online content – perhaps circulating to a mailing list of selected clients or prospective clients, sharing the content on social media – and then leaving it there, gathering metaphorical online dust. Law firms need to be actively engaging with that content *after* it has been shared with the wider world, as well as beforehand.

All online content is busy generating data. This data needs to be harvested, analysed, and used to influence future content. It can generate extremely valuable data-driven client insights. But how do you achieve this?

Continually assess the web analytics and review the content on your website that the audience is engaging with. Use cookies to identify who is engaging, and then tailor your content to engage further with them. Look at who does not appear to be engaging – was this the target readership, and what went wrong?

Look at the analytics provided by LinkedIn. Use your internal web experts to tell you what is being read most and shared most. Who is reading it, and who is sharing it? Is it other lawyers? General counsel? Are they based in the UK or internationally?

Ensure that data is regularly gathered and analysed from any interactive web applications, and key statistics fed back to the relevant teams.

Also ensure that content links to the biography of the relevant author. Lawyer biographies account for 80 per cent of law firm web site traffic, and are read more than 300 per cent more than any other page on a firm's site.[4]

And then it *almost* goes without saying that what is learned from this analysis can then be fed back into the next round of client-facing knowledge products generated by the team.

Conclusions

In *The Changing Role of the Professional Support Lawyer* (2008), Humphries suggests that "by simply referring to the client-facing PSL role, rather than focusing on the business development role, a PSL might place a dangerous emphasis on client-related knowledge activity at the expense of other internal knowledge activity which may, for some practice groups and firms, provide an even greater business benefit."

I would argue that there is, in many cases, only a limited difference between client-related knowledge and core knowledge activity, especially where efficiencies are identified and time is not spent reinventing the wheel.

As we have seen, the large body of specialist expertise amassed by the third-generation PSL can be used efficiently, tailored adeptly and disseminated widely, with the relevant data carefully examined. This will feed a process of continual improvement in the way that the team engages with its current and prospective clients.

References

1. Humphries, J. (2008) *The Changing Role of the Professional Support Lawyer*, ARK Group.
2. Susskind, R. (2017) *Tomorrow's Lawyers: An Introduction to Your Future* (2nd ed., Oxford University Press).

3. Nielsen, J. (2006) "F-Shaped Pattern for Reading Web Content", https://www.nngroup.com/articles/f-shaped-pattern-reading-web-content-discovered/
4. Pernice, K. (2017) "F-Shaped Pattern of Reading on the Web: Misunderstood, But Still Relevant", https://www.nngroup.com/articles/f-shaped-pattern-reading-web-content/

Chapter 5: The role of the PSL navigating legal tech and document automation

By Clare Harman Clark, senior PSL at Taylor Wessing

For a profession so inherently reliant on harnessing the nimble ingenuity of the human mind, it's perhaps unsurprising that moves by the legal industry to embrace *artificial* intelligence have been, at best, tentative. Lawyers may be creatures of considerable intellect, but they are not the dynamic innovators of tech start-ups. They are the product, workplace-wise, of careful habit – they are not industry disruptors.

Lawyers are also not daft, of course – many will remember when the letter gave way to the email. The manageable meander of physical correspondence bobbed about a bit and then went under in the wake of vast inboxes. Instant messages soon demanded instantaneous responses. The "cc" address created fast-moving accountability and destroyed the notion of ever being offline. The rest, as they say, was perpetually interrupted weekends.

Still, if some reticence towards new technology is understandable, the real problem today is that *legal tech* – that catch-all pot into which AI is deposited – is pretty nebulous; it covers a multitude of things.

Take the average, technically-savvy team member. This lawyer is at one with their work-issue iPhone. They trust in the storage and search functionality of the virtual file over the hard copy lever-arch. They confidentially manipulate PowerPoint and actively engage with LinkedIn. But did they know, for example, that the ever-expanding data sets that law firms produce *every day* lend themselves to fledgling machine processing technologies?

They did not, they mutter politely, *how fascinating*.

In the not-too-distant future, machine learning will surely revolutionise the future provision of legal services, you say, cutting out the need for repetitive and time-consuming (and potentially error littered) due diligence drudgery. Soon, a scanner will put paid to weeks of manual close-reading: a computer can devour a complex commercial lease portfolio, or report on the terms and conditions of an Amazonian workforce, in a single afternoon.

Really? They are probably already glancing, glassy-eyed, to their watch. They are calculating lost billable time in the now, let alone in some esoteric future. But don't let that stop you. Sure, the initial investment sounds expensive, and there are unanswered questions about the development of a new generation of trainees who will never undertake that apprenticeship at the coalface, but this technology is cutting-edge. You've read some fascinating articles.

And yet, by the time you have even mentioned impending click-button blockchain conveyancing and contract creation, it is too late.

They have already left.

Your smorgasbord was not just hard for a non-expert to engage with meaningfully, but it also feels potentially rather unappetising, given the immediate demands of the business at hand. Little surprise, then, that it rarely tempts those who will otherwise chew through the considerable fat of nineteenth-century case law.

At this stage, legal tech is only truly appealing when it responds to tangible, quantifiable business needs and firms with any appetite to pick 'n' mix from the products on offer are often therefore drawn to document automation. This electronic assembly process, which turns a series of transaction specific questions into custom-tailored first draft documents, has the genuine ability to make the business of law smoother, more consistent and more efficient.

Done well, document automation can offer real benefits. It lets fee earners produce a suite of documents within minutes. It cuts down on the risks of reusing old drafts; it slashes time spent proof-reading; and it ensures that documents look and feel the same, creating confidence in the firm's brand. Perhaps most excitingly, in the context of this book, it is not actually *artificial* intelligence in the truest sense. Once the software is installed, the process of turning a flat document into an automated one relies heavily on human, legal intelligence. In this way, it gives real opportunities to PSLs with an appetite for innovation and project management to stretch their roles, develop their skill sets, and add significant value to their firms.

Establishing the project

PSLs are a natural fit to contribute significantly to, or even oversee, a firm or department's shift to automation. Without (generally speaking) being experienced in project management, or particularly well-versed in IT, they nonetheless bring an invaluable perspective to the process. As the traditional gatekeepers for a firm's precedent banks, they are uniquely placed within the organisation of a law firm to ensure the project's success. Yet as

PSLs emerge from the back-office function of drafting, their deep knowledge means they are able to provide a robust bridge between software provider and end user (fee-earner). As they get increasingly involved in client relationships, they can identify tailored uses and opportunities that add real value to the law firm's offer.

However, we first have to get the project off the ground.

Board champions

Technological advances may be inching us slowly towards a far, far better place, but – in the meantime – their ability to inspire managerial support and meaningful budget within the current financial year can be lacklustre. Document automation is a costly business. Firstly, there is the product purchase and dedicated hours selecting and coding precedents; in the longer term, the firm is committing to paying for technical support – training for users, software upgrades, etc.

Whether these costs are paid to external providers or an in-house team, they still need to be anticipated and met – ideally centrally. If a project like automation is approached in such a way that anticipates allocating cost and skills too specifically to departments, it's hard to envisage many of those departments offering to lead. This is a project that benefits the entire firm, and with clients increasingly keen to see their advisers work in a way that avoids practice area silos, it is a backward step to devolve technological capability.

Board-level champions are therefore essential. They will release the budget, but also their vocal support will keep the project on track and set a tone of engagement through the organisation. It is a mindset – a direction of travel – and it cannot be underestimated. The cultural shift to a tech-led workplace simply cannot start from the bottom up; a law firm committed at its highest levels to engaging with legal tech is best placed to make the most of the document automation product.

Identifying the value

Unsurprisingly, the creation of a compelling case for automation technology is a far simpler exercise in retrospect. At the outset of the board's consideration, unless it is full of lawyers who've had the benefit of document automation elsewhere, it might be difficult to convey the ease with which an entire suite of transaction-specific documentation can be created. Once up and running, a five-minute demonstration may speak louder than words, but in the meantime it is vital to link the project intimately with desired business outcomes.

Too often, when legal tech takes on its own momentum, driven by its products' own capability rather than its users' needs, IT *solutions* are gifted before fee-earners actually had a chance to identify a problem. The new products, no matter how complex, can get easily side lined as lawyers, who rely for excellence on tried and tested working routines, will not break with habit without considerable persuasion.

Before approaching the board therefore, make sure you have done grass-roots investigation amongst your colleagues and that you don't promote solutions unless they link intimately to your firm's practice objectives.

Ask the same questions of everyone who might ultimately use the automation product to understand what they need.

Ask questions about document production

- How do you create a new document?
- Which part of producing a document is cumbersome, repetitive or time consuming?
- What impact, hypothetically, might automated documentation have on your quotes for fee earning work?
- What percentage of non-fee earning work or what processes would benefit from automation?
- Where are the most mistakes/typos made?
- What benefit is there to consistency of approach amongst fee earners?
- How do fee earners find guidance and know how when they draft documents?
- What approaches have any clients made to ask about our firm's adoption of legal tech? what do you think clients now expect?
- What could make your lives easier?

Admittedly, it may be hard to extract genuine opinions and feelings from exercises such as these. Your colleagues may be keen to share, they may not. They may be suspicious of change or they may be desperate for it. They may know nothing, or everything, about the products out there. Listen carefully to what you are told: encourage clarity (if "some processes could be automated" – which ones?) and try and resolve contradictions (if "I can never find relevant know-how" is voiced, then "I think the current system works well" cannot be entirely true).

Lastly, remember not to lead your colleagues towards predetermined answers. Ask open questions to avoid unhelpful yes/no answers and don't be concerned whether the answers given point inexorably to the introduction of documentation software or not. At this stage, the most important thing is to identify the real needs of your department or your firm. It is only when armed with these answers that you might be able to achieve the cultural and budgetary support required.

There's no I(T) in team

Assuming the board has granted its support, remember even the most IT-enthusiastic PSL will not undertake an automation project in isolation. Key to this the size and scope of team is, of course, cost. Still, you might think laterally and draw from outside the no-doubt stretched IT department. Are there people within your organisation with skills or experience that lend themselves to involvement in the project? How much (spare) budget is there for IT training? Is there enthusiasm to harness in return for project management training?

What timescales are anticipated from project launch to full precedent automation? No self-respecting board will agree to an amnesty on normal legal work while the automation project is established. Given the ongoing demands of department and firm therefore, what bolt on cost may be required for peripatetic coders?

Is there sufficient skillset in-house to support the automation product once it is up and running, or will you need to sign up to ongoing support packages moving forward, whether in order to integrate software with existing products, or simply to support its daily use? Plan for a team (even in the loosest sense) that flexes with the demands of the project and maximises the skills the law firm is able to develop and retain in-house.

Product selection

Before you invite software providers in to showcase their wares, make sure you know what exactly you are looking at. As with any project, compile a realistic needs assessment, one that sits comfortably with the answers to your investigation.

You might start with a brainstorm grouping desired outcomes, but end with a strict chart, grading wants and needs relative to business need. Create categories to make sense of the differing features of the products in the market place:

- "*Must have*: red lines that will make the project stand or fall";
- "*Should have*: fairly expected deliverables"; and, lastly

- "*Nice to haves*: features that can be sacrificed if they affect the ability to deliver others".

Undertake a formal cost-benefit analysis to assess the anticipated benefits against the product specific costs and the results may surprise you. At this stage of stepping into the unknown, frankly, even the most back-of-a-deeds-packet return on investment calculation might be the best you can achieve numerically, but you can make educated judgement calls on how a software offer will integrate with your firm. The things you thought were a red line for proceeding with the project may, in the context of other features on offer, be demoted to nice to haves.

Once you have made your product selection, the hard work can begin.

Coding the precedent

Consider your department's workflows and select a precedent that is widely used. Then, from the outset, the physical act of automating a document means learning to see it not as a flat page of text but as logical workflow.

Key to automation is the user questionnaire that front ends every lawyer's engagement with the product. Ultimately, the user will launch the software, select the desired template and immediately face a series of questions you have designed as pertinent to the transaction in hand. The information captured here will determine the shape and content of the first draft they obtain.

The questionnaire should reflect a dynamic decision tree, where each branch represents real world options, sensibly structured around the predictable end user questions:

- Who are your parties?
    - How are the parties referred to?
    - What information are you compiling in relation to them?
    - What information is held already, and could be third party checked?
    - What specific execution requirements can you insert?
- What are you doing?
    - List *all* of the transaction documentation that can be anticipated and generated.

- When are you doing it?
  - Peg completion and effective dates to transaction milestones.
  - Deal with conditionality and formalities (pre- and post-)
- How will it happen?
  - Structure your questions so they make sense chronologically in the life span of the transaction.
  - Insert financial/tax calculations where relevant.
  - Ask about relevant supplemental documentation at the right time.

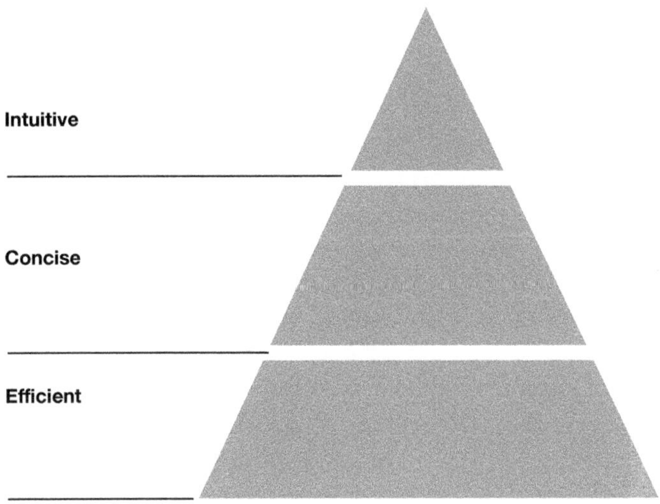

Figure 1: The ICEberg

More specifically, when designing the questionnaire, keep an **ICE**berg in mind. Your questions must be:

- **Intuitive** – Our iceberg's slippery pinnacle must be one-size-fits-all; your automation will inevitably be used by new trainees and highly experienced partners. With this in mind, it is vital that your questions are intuitive, and empathetic to the user.
  - Do not reference esoteric concepts.
  - Avoid statutory references that need to be looked up.
  - Group questions by sense, so you are not jumping about on the timeline of a transaction or between different legal disciplines relevant to it.

- **Concise** – Putting "concise" in the slowly spreading middle of the 'berg highlights how challenging it is. In striving to be brief, it is easy to become obscure.
    - Consider if you can safely assume information from the answers already inputted.
    - Be careful how you include alternative drafting options; maybe put these in optional footnotes where they risk bogging down the questionnaire with too many questions or too much complexity.
    - Set a target time for your fee earners to complete the questionnaire, and test it constantly. There will be a tipping point in minutes taken after which it is quicker for them to rehash a previous draft than start afresh with your new automated precedent. At that point, they will abandon the product.
- **Efficient** – Ensure every single one of your questions works hard behind the scenes. A party's name will appear on, *inter alia*, the front page, the execution blocks and the notices provisions, but can you defend an intricate enquiry on the tax history of an asset on the same terms? Try and reduce the necessary data entry – at both ends of the process. Ask yourself: how important is the answer to this question? Will it mean that four out of five of your suite of documents are neater and tailored, or just one? Does it mean various clauses can be dispensed with as the draft is assembled, or are we just talking about one word?
    - Allow the questionnaire to concertina out so only relevant questions are asked.
    - Consider whether the user is realistically able to answer the question in hand at the outset of a transaction. Forget how transactions *ought* to be run; a lot of information (as you know from your time in practice) is only acquired later.
    - Take a consistent approach to all the precedents, so users learn the language and anticipate the information they will need. Chose a party title, for example, and stick to it – don't ask for the name of a "funder" in one document where elsewhere you use "lender" or "bank", or "chargee". Decide upon "surety" or "guarantor". Differences between departments can be highlighted in this process, making them easier than normal to fix for a cohesive firm output.

Depending on the product, you may have the option to create separate guidance panels in the questionnaire to help the user select the right answer. These can be helpful but do use them advisedly. This guidance might only be needed by a fee-earner once, so try and avoid leaving it hanging around to clutter the questionnaire page indefinitely. Moreover, if the information it contains is really important, or liable to change as a transaction progresses, it might be better to put it in the document as a footnote at the appropriate point so that it remains visible to the lawyer for longer.

Your precedent is now a process and needs – behind the scenes – to cater for all of the real-world scenarios that your team might commonly encounter. Rather than a necessarily rather long-winded description of a transaction, think of the automated document as a *choose your own adventure* book. This process is about more than dropping client names into an existing precedent template. PSLs have a helicopter view of the work a team does and are uniquely placed to pre-empt this. If your real estate team does a lot of work for a high street retailer, for example, include the ability to pre-populate the appropriate definition of "use" in a lease. If your finance team produces charging documents for a particular lender, incorporate its preferred terms.

Of course, the act of "coding" the document for the software is a technical one. But just as it may be unrealistic to expect you to become an expert coder, the expert coders are not, for the most part, expert legal drafters. The result of this is that it is vital to work very closely with your coding team, in-house or external, to make sure that the nuances of your question are properly translated into the selection of clauses or sentences.

Testing, testing...

So – you have compiled the most legally astute precedent, and broken down your department's transactions into a fluent series of steps, each surefooted on the ICE. With technical alchemy, the coders have turned your work into fully functional document automation. What must happen next, before the flurry of launch excitement, is a period of testing.

Very few people like to be tested. Even fewer people have time to undertake testing. With the best will in the world, asking fee earners to squeeze an opportunity from their days to stress test the system from the comfort of their own desks is unlikely to end well. Yet still, it is vital that the automated processes are tested, and not only to save them from the typo-blindness that your staring at the drafts for days might by now have invoked. As well as your questions may have been formulated, it is vital to see how another person approaches them; to realise what happens when they misinterpret a phrase or insert something you might not have expected.

From experience, it is sensible to set up time-limited, tightly-controlled tester sessions away from your colleagues' normal desks. Book a training room with equipment and encourage the broadest range of fee-earners to attend. Hand out hypothetical transaction scenarios (maybe containing all the necessary information, maybe not). Ask your colleagues to complete the questionnaire alone (and give feedback on this) and generate a document.

Factor in sufficient time and budget between testing and go-live to actually resolve issues and implement solutions. You can then go through the documents produced, to be clear that every sentence that ought to have been generated, does in fact appear. This will give you the best sense of whether the automation has worked both for the precedent and for your team.

Managing the cultural shift

Change and disruption is hard. It makes most of us anxious, particularly when it approaches rapidly, cloaked in unfamiliar, technological language, screaming promises of breakneck transaction speed. It is easy to dismiss the emotional cost of uncertainty, but ultimately it will be harder to ignore when the usage figures are finally generated for your finished product. If fee-earners are not comfortable using the system, it will not become the success you or the board are hoping for.

Undoubtedly, the key to positive and active engagement from your department and your firm is communication.

Monitor and report on performance

With so much work behind-the-scenes complete, you will surely announce automated precedent launches with an appropriate fanfare; however, remember to report regularly on the system moving forward. Measure quantifiable good news statistics: the number of documents automated, the savings in time and effort compared to the previous approach to document production, the opportunities for data capture/checking, the consistency of practice, and the increasingly diverse in-house skillsets. You might even be able to generate a sense of the environmental benefit of the automation system given reduced paper wastage.

Respond actively to any engagement

Encourage your users to speak openly about whether the end product meets their needs and delivers on their expectations. If the process isn't actually working against those outset objectives, be nimble enough to change the path you are on.

The inherent beauty of automation software is in the (relative) ease with which it can be manipulated. Fix an erroneous reference in one document, and the entire transactional suite can be updated at the click of a button. A rogue typo is corrected in seconds. Colleagues who actively engage must be thanked, and they will become ambassadors for the product.

By encouraging your colleagues to be a vital part of the testing process early on, you will engender a sense of shared ownership that can only improve the quality of the precedent bank overall. It is a recurring bugbear of PSLs that fee-earners must be bribed (if not actively poked) to share thoughts and ideas and experiences on the use of a firm's precedents. With this process, they will start to see the template as you now see it, and their confidence will increase. The precedent itself is not sacrosanct; it is a tool – robust and formidable, of course, but still, at heart, a jigsaw piece to be manipulated to suit each transaction and each client's needs.

Articulate the value of legal tech

In the column inches of a sensationalist media, AI is just one more unsolicited IT solution, amounting to nothing more than the inexorable rise of the machines, and an inevitable jobless dystopia. Ultimately, however, the great prize of well-executed machine automation is in freeing up the lawyers for the tasks that require more intuitive cognitive skills. Employment in the financial services may have suffered as processes moved online, but the legal world and the current capacity of legal tech is different. The process of negotiation will not – any time soon at least – fall prey to the automation software. The nuances of creating current and future leverage, of anticipating legal developments while preserving the client's delicate commercial relationships is still a step – if not a country mile – off.

In this context, the role of automation as merely processing the input information is less about laying waste to the legal world as we know it, and more about freeing up its valuable time; giving it the space and the billable hours to flourish. This distinction is crucial and it must, with the engagement of the supportive board, be stressed.

So while legal tech conversations are almost certain to veer into unchartered territory – peering at new forensic accounting software or across online platforms for sharing legal self-help, or even veering towards the "there be witches" chat about robotic paralegals – there is a fantastic role for the PSL able to maximise the possibilities and provide genuine solutions to outdated and inefficient legal practice. A document automation project highlights the value of applying a PSL's significant legal practice expertise and knowledge to off-the-shelf technological solutions.

And, ultimately, this is a brave new world worth exploring.

Chapter 6: The evolution of the PSL role – a case study from the employment world

By Charles Pigott, PSL at Mills & Reeve LLP

As the Danish philosopher Søren Kierkegaard remarked, it is often said that life can only be understood backwards, but people forget to add that it has to be lived forwards.[1] That explains why it is probably only as a result of reflecting on the past 17 years working as an employment PSL that I'm now in a position to understand how my career has developed. It follows that I need to open this chapter with the obvious caveat: past experience is not necessarily a guide to how the role may develop in the future. However, for reasons that will be explained, I believe it is a fair assumption that many people embarking on a PSL role now will be presented with comparable choices and opportunities.

Starting out

The world was a different place when I started out as a PSL in 2001 after nearly 20 years in private practice. I was the first PSL to be appointed in Mills & Reeve's employment, pensions and immigration team, and the fourth overall in the entire firm.

There is no need to reiterate what has changed since then in any detail. However, it is worth recalling in this context that I joined several years before Twitter was founded (2006) or the first iPhone launched (2007). Both of these developments have had a transformative effect on the way knowledge is shared, but I plan to concentrate instead on the ingredients of the role that have remained relatively constant.

As the job title suggests, the most important element of the role remains to provide support to the so-called front-line lawyers in your particular discipline. How that support is provided will change depending on what happens in the relevant areas of law, and the technology and published sources available. It will also depend on the human and financial resources available to the team being supported.

In my case, my arrival at Mills & Reeve (where I have spent my entire PSL career) coincided with favourable economic conditions and a Labour government that was promoting a good deal of new employment legislation. This was partly due to their domestic agenda, but it was also attributable to the need to implement a number of EU directives in the employment field.

I joined at the point when case law was only beginning to emerge on legislation like the Working Time Regulations and the National Minimum Wage, Data Protection and Human Rights Acts (all dating from 1998). In the pipeline were major changes to anti-discrimination legislation, which led to the outlawing of workplace discrimination based on sexual orientation and religion in 2003, followed by age in 2006. There were also significant changes over this period to the rights of part-time and fixed term workers, also due to EU legislation.

When I made the move from private practice I knew no more about these emerging areas of law than the lawyers I was supporting. But what I did have in my new role was dedicated time to follow these developments and work out the best way of sharing knowledge about them. In those days there was little material of any quality available free on the internet, and many specialist subscriptions had not yet moved online. In addition, while the Practical Law Company had been launched, it did not yet have an employment offering

In the first few years in the job I spent more time analysing and writing about new developments than I do now, particularly because there was a longer time lag between legislation being published and the first publicly available analysis appearing. However, the way this information was communicated was relatively straightforward. Social media was in its infancy and there was greater reliance on know-how data bases, e-mail and face-to-face communication.

Had I started in my job 10 years later, I suspect I would have had to go through the same process to gain knowledge and establish credibility. However, there would have been more emphasis on editing and customising existing material, and following and sifting material on social media channels. I would also have had to spend more time working on more efficient and innovative ways of sharing this information internally.

Similar considerations apply to another core element of my role – maintaining precedents. Our lawyers did not have ready access to a bank of externally drafted precedents, or at least one that was easy to use. I therefore had to dedicate a fair amount of time to assessing the precedents we were already using across the firm and working out how they could be rationalised and kept up-to-date. These days the tools used would be different – for example, many firms deploy their core precedents using specialised document assembly software, rather than maintaining Word templates, and rely on subscription sources for those that are less frequently used.

However, in my experience, the core analytical skills required remain much the same, particularly when one considers how document assembly software – often misleadingly referred to as document automation – actually works in practice.

Becoming an expert

A few years into the job, I acquired a degree of knowledge in some corners of employment law, which enabled me to support my team in additional ways. Rather than simply being a facilitator to help the spread of knowledge, I became a sounding board for colleagues who wanted to explore how a new piece of legislation applied to a particular problem they were grappling with. I also had the chance to do a limited amount of client work.

The age discrimination legislation, which was introduced in the employment field in 2006, provides a good example of how this happened. The law in relation to age discrimination differs in a number of important respects from other strands of discrimination law that had been introduced before – for example, in relation to sexual orientation or religion or belief. For one thing, everyone in the workplace was potentially protected, since it did not apply only to discrimination against older people, but also to less favourable treatment because you were thought to be too young. In addition, unlike other discrimination strands, direct discrimination on ground of age is not inherently unlawful. In those days there was a specific exemption for imposing compulsory retirement age. In addition, other kinds of direct discrimination could (and still can) be justified as a "proportionate means of achieving a legitimate aim".

Since no one had considered issues like this before, it enabled me to acquire a degree of expertise in my own right which was useful to the firm. Of course, I could not know as much about the nature of each client's business as my colleagues who worked with them regularly, but I probably had a better grasp of how these new requirements had been shaped and how they were likely to be interpreted.

The Labour party lost power in 2010, and the employment policy of the Coalition Government was very different. However, from my point of view, the outgoing Labour Government left one important legacy: the Equality Act 2010. This came into force shortly after the Coalition came into power.

The Equality Act brought together under one roof almost all Great Britain's previously scattered discrimination legislation (Northern Ireland still retains the old piecemeal structure of equality legislation). By doing so, it moved equality issues up the agenda as well as making a number of significant changes to the law. The Act also changed our perspective internally, as it encouraged links between our employment lawyers and other lawyers of the firm where discrimination law was relevant to their practice. That, in turn, gave me an opportunity to look more broadly at discrimination law, and to collaborate and share information with lawyers outside the employment practice.

Spreading your wings

The Coalition Government may have agreed to implement the Equality Act (with some relatively minor exceptions), but it was never going to be as wholehearted about extending employment rights. Indeed, in its early years it flirted with abolishing the right not to be unfairly dismissed entirely. In the end it settled on increasing the qualifying period, reducing the maximum compensation, and introducing compulsory early conciliation for most employment claims.

However, to say that the Coalition Government and the majority Conservative Government which followed it was not interested in legislating for the workplace would be an oversimplification. For a start, it was the first government for many years to be prepared to change trade union law, in particular by tightening the rules on industrial action ballots. It also brought in the apprenticeship levy and introduced gender pay reporting. However, at least for my firm's practice, these changes were relatively peripheral compared to what had gone before.

The two most significant legal developments I have had to grapple with in the past few years have come from outside the mainstream employment field. The first, the General Data Protection Regulation that took effect in May this year, is a piece of directly effective EU legislation. The second is, of course, Brexit, a slowly unfolding process triggered by the success of the leave campaign in the 2016 referendum. Both of these are huge topics which span many different disciplines.

Because no one person can fully get to grips with either topic, these developments have given me the opportunity to broaden my knowledge and to collaborate with a much greater range of people across the firm.

Taking Brexit as an example, the referendum had an immediate impact on EU workers in the UK, many of whom felt unsettled and unsure of their future. A number of our clients – particularly in the health and education sectors – needed our support to understand the legal implications and what steps they could take to support their workforce. This has given me the opportunity to follow the Brexit process closely – from the EU (Notification of Withdrawal) Act 2017 through to the EU (Withdrawal) Act 2018 and beyond – and to consider how these and associated developments are likely to affect EU nationals exercising their freedom of movement rights in the UK.

As my knowledge in this area developed, I had more to contribute to our firm-wide Brexit capability and have ended up editing the dedicated Brexit pages on Mills & Reeve's website, as well as being part of the group that decides on what other Brexit-related information we should be sharing externally.

Looking to the future

I don't think my area of practice is atypical. In most corners of the law, there are periods of intense activity and periods of consolidation where the most significant legal developments may come from outside your specialist practice area. These present different opportunities, but during a typical career PSLs are likely to experience both phases of what I think can be seen as an inevitable, if unpredictable, cycle.

Much has been written about the possibility that artificial intelligence will supplant many of the traditional PSL jobs. While I'm sure that they will continue to evolve – as my own experience demonstrates – I am confident that there will always be a role for PSLs, or something very similar.

I have largely steered clear of technology in this case study, as I have decided to focus on the legal content of the job rather than the way the content is assimilated and shared. However, I wanted to end with a quick experiment I did with Google Translate – a potential job disrupter if ever there was one – when preparing to write this chapter.

When checking the correct translation of the Danish original of Kiergergaad's famous aphorism, it offered me this:

> *"One is quite true, what Philosophy says, that life must be understood as the backlogs. But above all you forget the second phrase that it must be lived out of date."*

I certainly understand backlogs, and my children would say that my private life is lived out of date, but it certainly isn't what Kierkegaard meant. If he was right, we can only understand the impact of new technologies in retrospect, and claims for what they might achieve in the future need to be met with a healthy degree of scepticism.

Reference

1. Det er ganske sandt, hvad Philosophien siger, at Livet maa forstaaes baglænds. Men derover glemmer man den anden Sætning, at det maa leves forlænds (It is perfectly true, as the philosophers say, that life must be understood backwards. But they forget the other proposition, that it must be lived forwards.) Journals IV A 164 (1843) Cited at https://en.wikiquote.org/wiki/S%C3%B8ren_Kierkegaard (accessed 28/08/18)

Chapter 7: Managing PSL workload

By Karen Battersby, director of knowledge and learning & development at Charles Russell Speechlys

Scope of the PSL workload

The nature of the PSL role can be extremely wide-ranging, depending upon the KM priorities of the firm or practice group that the PSL works for. In the current climate of change in the legal profession, this range of activity is only increasing with the advent of new technologies and techniques – such as AI, document automation, process mapping, etc – which PSLs now need to consider to support their practice.

Most PSLs have a workload that can be split between projects – such as writing new precedents or implementing IT tools that facilitate the efficiency of their fee-earners' work – and "business as usual" (BAU) activity, such as helping with fee-earner enquiries, keeping people up-to-date with legal developments, facilitating know-how sessions, etc. Much BAU activity can be focused towards helping individuals with particular issues, which is a valuable part of the PSL role. However, too much time spent on BAU and helping individuals can distract the PSL from carrying out valuable strategic projects which benefit groups of fee-earners as a whole. There is also a virtuous circle that can be achieved by ensuring that sufficient time is allocated to the more substantial knowledge projects which result in the reduction of individual queries as well – for example, writing comprehensive practical guidance on a new development. Whilst it is human nature to deal with ad-hoc pieces of work and queries as they come in, this can cause real problems in KM if it means that the PSL cannot carve out sufficient time to create shared knowledge resources, which benefit a wider demographic than just those seeking help. Indeed, a reactive approach can result in a proliferation of the same issues being repeatedly raised by different individuals, without the resultant learning being shared.

Managing perceptions of the PSL role

Given the regular ongoing demands of the PSL role, it is important that fee-earners understand the mix of responsibilities that the role entails and the time that the PSL must devote in order to cover all the bases. Without an understanding of the role and its priorities, fee-earners might assume that the PSL is there for a whole range of appropriate and inappropriate activities deemed "support". As mentioned, a constant demand for assistance with undefined, lower value activities can detract from the time needed to implement more critical strategic projects.

Getting fee-earners and other users of the services that PSLs provide to understand the role and its priorities is key to helping PSLs manage their workload. The most effective KM strategies are ones which follow and support the firm's or practice's business strategy, and clearly define how KM activities do so. Setting a KM plan out in a document not only gives some much-needed clarity to the PSL role, but can also provide the framework for a thought-through work schedule aligned to achieving business strategy. Alongside defining and communicating the PSL workload, in some firms the decision has also been made to change the title of PSL to practice development lawyer (PDL) or knowledge development lawyers (KDL) to better indicate to fee-earners the strategic practice development role they are undertaking.

The benefits of having a KM plan

As discussed, communication of the priorities and mix of work, along with the reasons behind them, is key to managing fee-earner expectations in relation to PSL services. A great way to help visualise and manage the workload – and, simultaneously, educate fee-earners on the objectives the PSL is seeking to achieve – is to draw up a KM plan for the PSL or practice group concerned and publish this out to the group. This should identify both the strategic KM projects for the year and the level of BAU activity that can be accommodated in the available time. The plan should include priority ratings and target timings (for projects and other deliverables) against each activity (see figure 1 below for an example).

[ ] KM PRIORITIES 2018/2019
UPDATED [ ]

No.	ACTION	COMMENTS	RESPONSIBILITY	TIMEFRAME	STATUS
INTERNAL KNOWLEDGE					
PRECEDENTS					
PRACTICE NOTES / CHECKLISTS					
PROJECTS					
TRAINING					

Figure 1: KM plan example

Another benefit of having a plan, which should be agreed at the outset of the year with partners in the relevant group and any central KM function, is that the act of drawing it up itself generates a discussion around the PSL's role and promotes understanding of the strategic value that the PSL is seeking to add. It is best to agree the plan with relevant partners in advance of general release, so that there is senior support for it and an understanding at the partner level of the benefits of a structured approach to KM. Partners who are unaware of the PSL's role can be amongst the largest users of a PSL for individual support – for example, undertaking individual research or BD support for them. A lot of this type of work could more appropriately be directed to trainees or junior lawyers, which also assists with the latter's own development. However, because partners may perceive the more senior PSL to be more efficient in completing the task, they can tend to look to the PSL for support first, which is why an understanding of the strategic KM projects at that level helps for easier conversations when reviewing where work should be placed! As owners of the business, partners will be interested in the effect of good KM on groupwide efficiency, realisation and profitability; this understanding is therefore important to manage their own personal use and time demands of PSLs.

Once agreed, a KM plan also sets a benchmark against which newly arising activities over the course of the plan period can be evaluated and prioritised. It helps the PSL explain to fee-earners the level of support for particular tasks, and what is or is not possible in relation to ad-hoc requests that might otherwise knock priority activities off course.

To prioritise different activities in the plan effectively, PSLs and those involved in KM should consider analysing the known and regular activities for the year via an "Important-Urgent" two-by-two matrix (see Figure 2). Activities and projects that fall in the unimportant and non-urgent category can be considered for delegation or simply not prioritised; those in the unimportant but urgent category are potential time-eating traps that should be delegated to those better suited to deal with them. Whilst important and urgent items will need to be given some priority, it is also important to deliberately reserve time for the important but non-urgent items, which are often longer term strategic priorities.

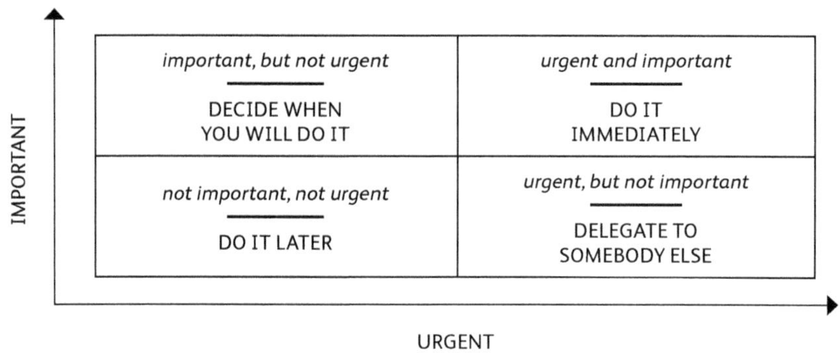

Figure 2: Important v. urgent matrix

Of course, whilst a KM plan should be used sensibly to set and communicate priorities and keep on track with goals, it is also important for the PSL to be pragmatic and sensible about accommodating minor "off plan" work that does not have a deep impact on achievement of the priorities, as part of the general support relationship with the practice group. The plan should be the subject of regular review and updating, particularly if the PSL and practice group agree to shift priorities so that original targets are moved back. My preference is to keep the original target in the plan but add notes as to the changes, so that when you are looking back at achievement over the year, the starting aims are clear – as opposed to having a constantly shifting plan.

Other techniques to manage PSL workload

Aside from having a clear and well-communicated plan of KM priorities, there are various other time and workload management techniques that can help PSLs manage their varied tasks and help set internal customer expectations about delivery.

"Surgeries"

To deal with ad-hoc enquiries during a busy period, the PSL could set up "surgery" times so that fee-earners know when is the best time to contact the KDL on general, non-urgent queries, which will then hopefully not spill into project work.

Carving out time and space

It is good practice for PSLs to be situated amongst the fee-earners they support to enable them to understand the work and issues for the practice, and facilitate knowledge-sharing more easily than if they are in a remote location. Some project work, however, such as drafting complex documents, requires head-down, uninterrupted concentration. It may therefore be useful to carve out periods of time for this when the PSL sits in a different location to avoid being overly disturbed. If the firm supports an agile working environment, some time might be allocated to doing this type of work at home.

Delegating KM work

Delegating drafting, training and research work to other appropriate fee-earners is part of the toolkit that a PSL should use to manage a heavy workload. Appropriate circumstances will be where the PSL is not expert in an area, but specialist fee-earners are, so they can be tasked with producing first drafts in those areas. Certain research might be useful to give to trainees, juniors or paralegals for a first cut and review by the PSL. Most firms recognise or have targets for non-chargeable or investment time by fee-earners, so allocating tasks to fee-earners to meet this requirement will also help them achieve these objectives. Equally, other departments like the library or information services team may be able to help with KM maintenance tasks, such as maintaining taxonomies and the categorising and tagging of knowledge documents in a KM system, which is within their area of specialist expertise.

PSL work, as with most disciplines, will involve some admin tasks – e.g. setting up training events – and some firms have invested in specific knowledge paralegals to supports PSLs with the organisational aspects of their role, so that they can spend more time on the pure KM work.

Making sure fee-earners are aware of the knowledge resources

After all the work has been put in to producing knowledge resources, it can be frustrating if they're not used and the PSL's time is taken up with queries that can be answered by reference to the resources. PSLs are therefore well advised to dedicate some ongoing time to promoting new and existing resources to fee-earners and pointing them in the direction of the knowledge collection to find the answers they are looking for. It can take some time for fee-earners to get used to accessing new resources rather than seeking individual help, but instilling a culture of using these as a first port of call will help the PSL manage their time and workload in the long run.

It has become more well accepted in legal KM, with the growth in sophisticated and targeted external knowledge resources – e.g. daily alerts from legal publishers – that PSLs should not spend too much time nowadays on replicating the detail of external current awareness that fee-earners can receive direct from those sources. It is more valuable for PSLs to be supplementing that resource with practical guidance on what steps fee-earners should take in the light of developments. If PSLs are subject to requests for detailed current awareness support, they can help fee-earners set up their own tailored external alerts to manage this aspect of the workload.

Saying "no" (and how to do it without damaging relationships)

There will undoubtedly be occasions when the PSL will have to say "no" to certain work requests. In order not to damage relationships with internal clients in this situation, and to take the opportunity to educate people on other sources of help available, it is best to deal with these situations by pointing the requester in the direction of the other resources. The PSL can also suggest time slots to assist that fit in with other priorities, so that the requestor is still supported in a way that minimises the impact on the PSL workload. This approach also facilitates the education of fee-earners as to where to turn for future requests.

Conclusion

It is the sheer variety of PSL work that can make the role stimulating and enjoyable, but that variety can also present challenges with workload management. Hopefully, with a bit of planning, clear explanation and communication around the role, and a pragmatic, customer-focused approach, PSLs can manage these challenges to their own and their internal clients' satisfaction.

Chapter 8:
PSLs and paralegals

By Amanda Hamilton, chief executive of the National Association of Licenced Paralegals

"Paralegals aren't properly qualified and have no place within my practice" – generally, this is the view of most PSLs and their senior managers. While this comment is partially true – there are clearly a number of graduates who can't find training contracts and are not fully qualified – it doesn't mean they can't provide support for PSLs and bring a range of benefits to a legal practice. Paralegals, by their very nature, are one of the best options to support the support staff in any firm.

While it is true to say that a paralegal may not be qualified in the same way as a solicitor, a paralegal is nevertheless an individual who is trained and educated to perform legal tasks and offer legal services. Not being a qualified solicitor, barrister or chartered legal executive means that they must not perform (unless authorised to do so) "reserved legal activities" (as defined by Section 12 of The Legal Services Act 2007), nor must they "hold out" to be anything other than paralegals. In other words, they must not give the impression or allow others to make assumptions that they are solicitors, barristers or chartered legal executives. On this point, transparency and clarity are key.

However, there are still a wide range of activities and support duties they can perform – and for many firms that layer of added expertise alongside or supporting the PSLs can make a considerable difference.

What can a paralegal do, and how can they be helpful to PSLs?

Generally, the answer is that, apart from reserved legal activities, there is a wide range of tasks that paralegals can perform. Even though reserved legal activities still remain the monopoly of solicitors or barristers, some of these are being eroded in practice. Others, such as the right to conduct litigation, can be overcome by the PSL giving authorisation to the paralegal to do so.

Utilising the services of paralegals with properly accredited qualifications and training can boost the economy of any solicitor's practice and be a positive benefit to PSLs. Whether employed within the firm, outsourced on an ad hoc basis, brought in to cover a particular project or staff absences, a paralegal workforce can boost productivity and reduce costs. They can often "get up to speed" much faster than non-paralegal support staff – a particular benefit if they are being brought in for a short project or to cover for a member of staff. Many have specialist expertise in particular areas that can be drawn on if needed, or can be used to offer additional services to clients. There are many ways a paralegal can offer support within the PSL team and enable the team to be more productive.

Once you have succeeded in finding the right paralegal to assist you, it is important to nurture and value their role if you wish to retain their services. It is sad but true that many paralegals feel as though they are not valued, and their expertise and what they can offer is not recognised. However, it may not be just the paralegals' feelings that are hurt by this. Indeed, disregarding paralegals as mere cannon fodder is dangerous and may have an adverse effect on the future role that solicitors and PSLs play in the legal services market.

To explain the above statement, it is necessary to understand the context of the legal services sector and why there has been a growth in paralegalism. With the virtual eradication of legal aid for all but the most urgent cases, a gap has opened in the legal sector. Few consumers are able to pay solicitors' and barristers' fees and have been forced to represent themselves in court. This has caused mayhem within the court system, with judges delaying hearings in order to ensure that the litigant is given guidelines on what to do and the correct procedure. Many judges, at their discretion, are now allowing NALP (National Association of Licenced Paralegals) paralegals the right of audience to represent a client, provided they are satisfied as to their affiliation with NALP and their competency to do so.

Filling this gap does not step on the toes of solicitors or PSLs, but instead complements what they do. At the lower end of the legal services market it may not be financially viable for solicitors' firms to offer assistance to the consumer on a pro-bono basis since this is unsustainable within the profession. Paralegals can fulfil this role by offering access to justice at a reasonable, and much lower, cost. Paralegals are gaining licences to practise and opening their own firms, so why shouldn't PSLs take advantage of this and use their services?

You may be thinking that the information you have just read isn't relevant to you; after all, you don't make the decisions about who to employ or who to outsource work to. However, by understanding how a paralegal may be able to help you and your team, what they can and cannot do, and how to ensure you choose that has the right qualifications, you are better positioned to make the case for the right type of additional support – should you and your colleagues need it.

Understanding that paralegals are no longer just would-be solicitors could mean the difference between surviving and thriving. Employing a team of competent paralegal lawyers to support the PSLs would clearly be a cost-effective move compared with bringing in qualified solicitors to perform the same roles. Similarly, employing or outsourcing work to paralegals to support solicitors in-house will complement the work that is already being undertaken and can positively enhance the professional support workforce.

Why is there such an increase in the number of paralegals, and why should PSLs utilise their services?

There are a number of reasons why the paralegal workforce has increased exponentially.

Firstly, the flooding of law graduates into the sector. This is due to the increase in institutions running the professional qualifications of the LPC and BPTC. In 1982 there were only four colleges offering the SFE (Solicitors' Final Examinations – the forerunner to the LPC); in 2001 there were 28, and in 2010, 42. Translating this to human terms means that there are vast numbers of graduates encouraged to go through the system without any hope of gaining full qualification because the competition for training contracts and pupillages is so great. Most end up as either paralegals by default or leaving the profession altogether.

Secondly is the cost of legal education to qualify into the conventional legal professions. With law degrees costing £9,000 a year and the professional qualification costing up to £16,000, prospective law students are now looking for alternative routes to qualification. The paralegal route meets this need.

Thirdly, the demand for access to justice at a reasonable cost. As aforementioned, this has been brought about by the withdrawal of legal aid.

What should PSLs look for in a paralegal? How to choose the right paralegal

To understand this, it is necessary to know a bit more about the history and growth of the paralegal sector. In 1987, the National Association of Paralegals (NAPL, as it was then known) was established. Before the role of PSL was fully established, NAPL's mission was to offer membership to those supporting solicitors within law firms and within commerce, industry, and the private and public sectors. It also developed training programmes to encourage, promote and develop the role and practice of paralegal support staff and represent the best interests of its members.

Over a period of ten years, the NAPL developed two qualifications. The first was a benchmark for those who had not gained a law degree; the second, as a result of referrals by The Law Society, was specifically aimed at law graduates who were not able financially to move forward in their chosen careers, or unable to gain training contracts to do so. These qualifications are now known as the Level 4 Diploma in Paralegal Studies and the Level 7 Diploma in Paralegal Practice.

In 2004, after consultation, NAPL published its strategic plan for the self-regulation of the paralegal profession by way of licensing, which was implemented in 2005. NAPL was restructured as "The National Association of Licensed Paralegals" (NALP) and commenced issuing licences to paralegals who could satisfy the criteria. This is now regarded as the benchmark in England and Wales for the qualified, experienced and dedicated professional paralegal practitioner.

Since 2010, NALP has been an awarding organisation regulated by Ofqual, the government body that accredits national qualifications in England.

One of the main arguments surrounding paralegals is that they are not regulated by statute. The government has clearly indicated that it does not want to create further statutory regulation within the legal services sector. Statutory regulation is where an organisation is checked by the government under an Act of Law. It is an offence to practice a statutorily regulated profession without being listed on the relevant register for that profession.

What is voluntary or self-regulation?

Where a profession is not governed by an Act of Law, they are often subject to voluntary regulation. Such regulation can be drawn up and enforced by any appropriate body within that professional sector but will often take the form of a "membership" body for the professionals operating in that sector.

The NALP's role in self-regulation

In theory, anyone can describe themselves as a paralegal (whether or not they have qualifications, experience or training), but ensuring that they are NALP paralegals means that you know you are engaging someone who has a certain level of training, qualification, insurance and experience. You are also able to check their qualifications on the NALP register. NALP also has strict codes of practice that every member has agreed to abide by to ensure that each member understands and adheres to the standards expected in the industry.

Since the paralegal sector does not come under any statutory regulation – unlike solicitors, barristers and chartered legal executives – paralegals have relied upon NALP to act as a self-regulatory paralegal membership body of the sector for over 30 years.

Why PSLs should ensure that their paralegals are NALP registered
There is an abundance of paralegals coming into the sector – so how can you be sure that they are the right person for the job? Ensuring that they are NALP registered means that you can be confident they have been vetted carefully by the foremost paralegal body in the UK.

The Licenced Paralegal Register (LPR)
NALP created the LPR two years ago. The opportunity to be on the register is given to all NALP members at every level. As a PSL you can now look for a paralegal specialising in a specific area of law, or perhaps a student to help with administration at a junior level. Utilising this resource, it is easy to be assured that a paralegal you are about to employ is NALP-registered. The LPR is readily accessible by the public for all these purposes.

Are reserved activities going to restrict PSLs using the services of a paralegal?

This really depends on whether PSLs outsource to paralegals or bring them in to work on a particular project. Any paralegal that is brought in as support staff will be under the umbrella (for insurance purposes) of the law firm. The PSLs can therefore authorise the paralegal to do anything they believe that paralegal is competent to do. This could be to go to court and represent a client or conduct litigation (both of which are reserved activities). If the paralegal services are outsourced, more care has to then be taken about what is required and specified in a contractual agreement. For example, it may be possible to outsource representing certain clients in court to a paralegal firm, as long as the courts are given notice in advance and are satisfied as to each individual paralegal's competency.

What about "holding out"?

As the paralegal profession is not statutorily regulated, it is vital that paralegals do not infer in any way that they are anything other than paralegal practitioners. This should be clearly specified on any business card, website, or other marketing information. To lay claim to be a lawyer, for example, may be misleading to the general public or prospective employer because the assumption may be that "lawyer" means "solicitor". However, it is not entirely wrong to utilise the description of "lawyer", provided it is pre-empted by the word "paralegal". Any holding out, whether intentional or not, is illegal.

Ultimately, as a PSL, if you use the services of a paralegal in relation to a client's case, the client should be made aware that it is a paralegal and not a solicitor who will be dealing with certain aspects of their case.

PSLs should not forget that the legal services sector exists to offer a service to consumers, whether individuals or businesses. They are the end users of such services, and therefore communication and transparency of information is essential.

Paralegals and PSLs in practice: case studies

NALP member case study example 1

B, a man in his mid-40s, gained a degree in another discipline and worked in a very high-profile job for 25 years. He always wanted to enter the legal profession, and so decided to change careers to qualify as a barrister. He successfully passed both the GDL and the BPTC. However, he was not able to find a pupillage in order to gain a tenancy which would enable him practise as a barrister. Six years later, he is working as a paralegal as head of a project team at one of the top 20 law firms in the country.

NALP member case study example 2

C, a woman in her 40s, decided to qualify as a paralegal and successfully completed the NALP Level 4 Diploma in Paralegal Studies. Afterwards, she attained a paralegal role in a criminal law firm. Once she gained three years' experience, she attained NALP Licence to Practise, she set up her own criminal defence firm and has been granted licensed access by the Bar Standards Board in order to instruct counsel directly. She now offers services to a number of law firms on a support staff basis, as well as handling her own cases. Her level of expertise and experience has been invaluable for the PSLs who have worked with her.

NALP member case study example 3

J found a job as a junior assistant to a solicitor after leaving school. She gained 15 years' experience and was promoted within the law firm. She applied for NALP Fellowship membership through the experiential route and now runs the litigation department of the firm.

Chapter 9:
What tech is best?

By Lucy Hall, senior PSL at Eversheds Sutherland

What is AI?

AI is everywhere. From driverless cars that use AI to decide how a car should react in certain scenarios, such as an obstacle getting in the way, to Google's AlphaGo robot, which has beaten some of the world's leading Chinese board game Go players. In medicine, AI is used to analyse X-rays with impressive consistency and accuracy.

AI is the simulation of human intelligence processes by computer systems and other machines. These include machine learning (i.e. the acquisition of data and rules for using the data), the use of rules to make conclusions, and an element of self-correction.

AI can consist of robotics, vehicles, image analysis, textual analysis and voice systems.

AI is "trained" by subject experts and AI "learns" from those experts. Legal AI is trained by experienced lawyers and PSLs.

What is legal AI?

Legal AI can consist of:

- **Contract analytics** – the review of a contract to automatically extract data points (e.g. in real estate, the terms of a lease) from multiple existing contracts which can be in any format. It can also be used to cross-check a document that is being worked on;
- **Legal data research** – locating relevant information and using historic data to recommend next steps;
- **Natural language processing** – where AI is used to understand meaning from the spoken or written word and then acts on those requests e.g. creating a first draft; and
- **Machine learning** – e.g. reviewing client specific behaviour and creating predictive analytics.

The development of AI is moving at a fast pace. Clients are now expecting higher quality and lower costs. Law firms are using AI to meet these demands in order to avoid losing business, and PSLs often play an integral role in testing and choosing the best legal AI for their law firms. Legal AI is most frequently used in relation to data and clause extraction from documents – e.g. from bulk document sets for due diligence or discovery purposes –but its application is growing rapidly.

What AI products are available for the legal industry? How are PSLs involved in product selection?

With the wide variety of legal AI products on offer, PSLs are often involved in testing, analysing and choosing which product is most suitable for their practice area. PSLs are often in the best position to train AI and teach it about legal concepts so that it provides the best possible service to their teams. PSLs also frequently act as advocates of AI to encourage the lawyers in their teams to make the best use of this continually evolving technology.

Ravn

Ravn is an AI software that can automatically read, interpret and summarise key information from documents and unstructured data. Ravn has been used by various law firms to assist with certain real estate matters. Ravn is a legal technology product which has created a system to analyse UK Land Registry title deeds to extract data and information in order to provide legal notices for the correct property owners.

This task is something that junior lawyers and paralegals would have carried out in the past and instead of taking hours, Ravn can complete the same task in a matter of minutes. AI can conduct numerous tasks cheaply, efficiently and accurately, which creates the opportunity for lawyers to work on more interesting matters. Real estate PSLs have often been involved in presenting this product to their teams and training the junior lawyers on how to use the technology. The impact of AI and the evolving role of the PSL are intrinsically intertwined.

Luminance

Luminance is a document analysis software that can process large, complex and fragmented data sets. It is particularly beneficial for M&A due diligence, commercial contract and real estate review exercises. Luminance uses pattern recognition and machine learning algorithms to read contracts and other legal documents in any language, and can automatically identify clauses and legal concepts. Its machine learning capabilities mean it constantly improves and develops with experience. PSLs teach Luminance based on their wealth of knowledge and experience in specialist areas. The more examples Luminance is shown, the more accurate it becomes, as this knowledge is retained for future projects.

This legal tech product increases efficiency and accuracy and, for example, can assist corporate lawyers working on mergers and acquisitions to review thousands of documents when analysing target companies in transactions.

This machine learning technology enables lawyers to, for example, quickly see the governing law clause within a contract and identify wording that differs from the norm. Indeed, a partner at Slaughter & May has stated that Luminance can halve the time spent on due diligence.[1] Luminance means that lawyers no longer need to spend time carrying out the least interesting part of the due diligence exercise and can focus on analysing the results which, ultimately, is what the client is most concerned with.

PSLs have been involved in the launch of Luminance in law firms and have taught the technology how to recognise certain clauses or legal concepts. PSLs also act as advocates within law firms to promote Luminance and encourage lawyers to use it on their projects in order to get the best results.

Kira

Kira is a market leader AI product that is used for document review. Kira is a software that can be applied to due diligence or contract analysis to spot trends and analyse issues across documents and export reader-friendly reports.

PSLs have been testing Kira, using it to review leases. It can provide a significant amount of time saving for due diligence exercises and is a popular AI tool.

Lex Machina

In the USA Lex Machina, a start-up acquired by Lexis Nexis in 2015, reviews data about court rulings to analyse types of filed cases and examine historic successes, which replaces work that is normally carried out by newly qualified lawyers. In the UK, the Civil Justice Council, which oversees civil courts, proposed to include an online court for consumers to deal with low-value money claims.

This product demonstrates the breadth of legal AI that is available. As a PSL, it is important that you are aware of what is available and keep up to date with developments to ensure that your team remains competitive and profitable.

Virtual assistants/brokers

Voice assistant systems, such as Siri, Google Now and Cortana, all use AI to make decisions based on your instructions.

Eversheds Sutherland has developed a virtual assistant AI tool which can provide administrative support to in-house counsel and other teams. It is like Siri for lawyers. Users connect to the virtual assistant and can request it to carry out activities using natural language. The virtual assistant is a broker, meaning that once it understands the intent of the user, it is able to instruct other systems to carry out the required activities.

This virtual assistant can free up legal teams by working on routine admin tasks, which enables them to focus on high-value work. It can access public data sources to create documents automatically, such as NDAs or standard contracts, and it can also collect and provide information. Through its versatile AI driven chat interface, it can help clients identify new functions and new routines to teach it, evolving its capability. This is an innovative development and Eversheds Sutherland's PSLs have been consulted on this project. We are currently considering how it could assist our specific teams as well as our clients.

How can law firms know what to invest in?

Pilots are essential in order for law firms to test out the numerous legal tech products that are available in the market. PSLs are expected to be involved in either running or participating in such pilots, as they have an acute understanding of the type of tasks their lawyers undertake. PSLs also have a good understanding of the impact or improvements that AI may have in relation to carrying out legal tasks or drafting documents for clients.

Structured pilots allow PSLs and law firms to evaluate the usability of the different types of legal tech in real time against the traditional processes currently in use.

When will law firms need to invest by to avoid being left behind?

Law firms are currently introducing technology, and PSLs are assisting with deciding which product would be most beneficial to the lawyers they support. However, are law firms moving quickly enough in comparison with other sectors? Are law firms meeting their clients' needs and expectations?

The current climate within some law firms is one of experimentation with AI, rather than a wholesale roll-out of products out across their offices. However, AI is such an area of growth that, whilst all law firms are investing in this journey, they must begin to take meaningful steps now or face significantly lagging behind their competitors in a few years' time.

How will AI make lawyers/law firms more efficient?

"The 2020s will be the decade of disruption," says Professor Richard Susskind, who is co-author of *The Future of the Professions: How Technology Will Transform the Work of Human Experts* (2015). There is an increasing demand from management, who control legal budgets, to reduce costs by taking advantage of the savings offered by technology.

Clearly, if AI can be used to carry out the more mundane tasks of junior lawyers, this will free up their time to conduct more technical and interesting work, which is where clients see the real value. This should filter up the lawyer hierarchy and create more efficient and experienced lawyers.

What do clients expect?

Clients are increasingly expecting lawyers to deliver work using AI, either for specific matters or as part of a firm's toolkit, in the selection process for panel appointments. A law firm's adoption of AI should significantly strengthen its relationships with clients by helping them to achieve greater efficiencies and deliver a more valuable service.

AI will help lawyers to increase revenue, reduce costs, maintain volume and demonstrate innovation, which will in turn assist with winning and retaining clients. AI will definitely lead to greater efficiency and will challenge existing revenue models. Clients expect their legal advisers to make the best decisions around innovation, working with third parties and challenging existing processes. Clients simultaneously expect their legal providers to use legal technology to drive efficiency and deliver high-quality legal advice.

Client service delivery is the motivating factor for law firms and PSLs to embrace AI and work together to deliver the best possible service to their clients and remain competitive in the legal market.

Online resources in law firms – what is available and how often are they used?

Online resources are key research tools and current awareness products that are essential to the role of the PSL in order to update the lawyers on legal and market developments. There is some debate at the moment as to which resources are worth investing in and whether or not one resource outperforms another.

Practical Law is a keen favourite, renowned for its clear and concise summary of many legal topics and is often used as a starting point for lawyers. Lexis Nexis PSL, however, provides in-depth analysis and is a fantastic resource tool which also delivers excellent legal and current awareness updates.

PSLs are consulted on what investments generally law firms should invest in and why (i.e. resources, technology and training). PSLs' opinions are invaluable in terms of guiding a law firm to make these decisions, and are pivotal in deciding the way in which budgets are spent and resources developed. PSLs, of course, also need to canvass the views of their partners and teams to see if there are any varying opinions.

The future – what will the legal tech world look like in five years' time?

AI will have a significant effect on future legal practice. The legal tech world is moving at such a rapid pace that it is essential for PSLs and law firms to keep up to date with developments and remain open minded and receptive to testing the legal tech that is on offer. Law firms won't be able to survive and successfully compete unless they partner with AI technology.

PSLs may need to train lawyers to acquire new skills in the future. Lawyers will need to be able to draft a document specifically tailored for AI review, for example. PSLs also need to teach legal concepts to AI products, such as Luminance, so that these technologies can evolve and develop and improve and refine their capabilities.

It is very helpful to discuss with the PSL network what types of legal tech other firms are looking into and to attend PSL conferences, where legal tech providers are often presenting and demonstrating their products. Such events are a great opportunity for PSLs to compare and contrast what is available on the market and make informed views to report back to their teams.

In five years' time, legal tech will be the norm and will cut out a significant amount of monotonous tasks carried out by paralegals and junior lawyers, enabling them to focus on the analysis and legal advice that their clients really value and appreciate.

Clients will also expect the investment in legal tech to flow through to their fees and will increasingly be looking for the most cost-effective quotes involving legal tech. PSLs will be increasingly required to work almost as tech advisers or testers for their law firms, providing their invaluable opinions on what legal tech is best. PSLs may also need to train the AI and be its advocate, as a way of encouraging their lawyers to utilise this new technology, so that it becomes the norm and is viewed as a user-friendly resource.

Conclusion

PSLs should embrace new legal technology and be ahead of the curve in order to be advocates for AI to the lawyers they work with. AI is re-defining the role of PSLs, who are increasingly called upon to comment on and participate in any pilot of AI and advise on how it will be of most use to the lawyers in their practice areas. PSLs will be instrumental in training the AI technology so that it constantly improves and develops.

In fact, the market is seeing new knowledge manager roles being created for qualified lawyers or PSLs who have a keen interest in legal technology/innovation to join the central knowledge management teams of law firms. The purpose of these roles is to implement legal technology solutions/products and be involved in the pilots of new technology products.

The introduction of AI into law firms definitely assists in the current climate, where clients increasingly expect transactions to be completed in shorter time frames with competitive legal fees. Efficiency and value for money are key, and clients will expect lawyers to invest in AI technology whilst continuing to deliver high-quality legal work. PSLs should equip themselves with knowledge about the various AI products on offer so they can usefully participate in any debate regarding legal tech and investment.

Reference

1. Croft, J. "Artificial intelligence closes in on the work of junior lawyers", *Financial Times* (2017). Can be accessed: https://www.ft.com/content/f809870c-26a1-11e7-8691-d5f7e0cd0a16

Chapter 10: PSLs and business development – converting current awareness into client engagement

By Julia Bateman, PSL at Kingsley Napley

When I was asked to contribute to *The Evolving Role of the PSL*, it gave me the opportunity to reflect on my own experience. Where do I make most of an impact, what is my "added value", and how does this compare to the experience of others in this part of the profession?

When I first attended the ARK professional support lawyers conference in 2015, some three months into my new job, it soon became clear to me that there was a whole spectrum of roles and a dizzying array of responsibilities in this field. Professional support lawyer; director of knowledge management and learning & development; global head of know-how – to name but a few! In some larger firms the roles are divided and clearly delineated; in others, a combination of the above. The conference certainly gave me food for thought and some helpful guidance on how to progress projects in my early days.

As I settled into my new role, I focused on building the precedent library, organising know-how provision, and consolidating and facilitating the cross-firm "communities of practice" – our "groups". I soon moved on to apply my own experience in relation to law reform and legislative developments to enhance the team's business development and marketing objectives. It is this aspect of the role that I will focus on in this article.

How I got here

Having started my career with a stint in the European Commission's new Justice and Home Affairs Directorate back in 2000, I then spent two years as advisor in the European Parliament before moving to, and then heading up, the Law Society's Brussels Office. This experience gave me a real understanding of the development of legal policy and legislation in its earliest stages and the advantages that knowledge of this can bring. It brought me into contact with forward-thinking practitioners who were active in the future of their discipline.

The ability to navigate opaque processes, retrieve draft legislation from clunky databases, and plough through parliamentary transcripts all lent itself to a good understanding of what was coming down the line and how to capture it. Moreover, I learned how to build relationships for influence in order to garner information that was not publicly available. It soon became clear to me that insight and intelligence are valuable commodities and a real must for leading practitioners in their field.

One element of this is that large corporates and organisations either have their own representations in Brussels or are heavily engaged in associations and networks. Lawyers who wish to service this client base need to be aware of the wider institutional and political landscape and the key players in the field – on top of knowledge of the specific legislative proposals that would impact on that particular sector. This was all before Brexit reared its ugly head... and monitoring EU developments and implications of the UK's withdrawal from the EU became a full-time job for some.

The big question at the time for me in terms of transmitting the information I had to the profession was how to attract the attention of busy practitioners with something that is not yet in force and not yet applicable. The answer: make it relevant to their day job. Bite-sized chunks of relevant information with an understanding of how it relates to client needs – a lesson I carry with me today.

It is worth reminding myself that the first time I became aware of the existence of professional support lawyers were via those I engaged with through our EU newsletters and European Court of Justice updates. Those who knew the value of the "forward-look" alerts as a key part of their own current awareness programme.

Effective knowledge management and the bottom line

For me, playing an active role in the delivery of current awareness means I must have systems in place to provide and share information on the "nuts and bolts" of criminal litigation. This includes amendments to criminal procedure rules and practice directions, substantive law developments in terms of draft legislation, legislation due to come into force, and landmark cases. It also includes the development and implementation of codes of procedure and protocols from law enforcement agencies and sentencing guidelines. In addition, this means keeping abreast of the current academic and practitioner debate in these areas. I work closely with our Knowledge and Information Services (KIS) team to constantly find ways to improve the provision of this information. This is alongside (the headache) that most of us in the knowledge management field face – how to develop a knowledge sharing culture amongst fee-earners via (for example) precedent libraries, handbooks and internal training, and regular know-how roundtables.

Capturing "tacit knowledge" – a well-worn topic in KM debate – appears to be the Holy Grail!

Much has been written on how effective knowledge management systems and systematic current awareness can contribute to business development through improved efficiency. The need for efficient knowledge management processes that are fit for purpose and meet the needs of busy practitioners – ultimately benefiting the "bottom line" by cutting costs – does not need to be rehearsed here.

What I would like to reflect on is how the work I undertake for current awareness and know-how can have an additional purpose in contributing to the strategic direction of the department and enable the fee earners to maintain and enhance their market leading position. Some of what I say will be modelled in other firms, and indeed PSLs and business development feature as a topic in the 2018 ARK professional support lawyers conference. What I wanted to do here is give live examples from my practice area and my particular portfolio of topics.

Knowledge is currency in business development

Many in my department are leading lights in their field so require little by way of input on technical expertise. They are heavily engaged in their wider practitioner community and hold leadership positions in many of the networks such as the Fraud Lawyers Association (FLA), International Bar Association, European Criminal Bar Association and London Criminal Courts Solicitors Association (LCCSA). They author practitioner texts and are the go-to people for media comment. This all consolidates their position in the market place; however, as with any sector, it is a competitive landscape. To maintain their position, practitioners not only need to excel in their legal counsel but be active and visible in the community – something that I therefore need to nurture and support.

It is up to me, then, to understand not only the firm and department business plan but each fee earner's practice and their interests. By ensuring that I am on top of the broader developments relevant to them, I can take action to ensure that this knowledge can be translated into marketing action and business development.

I support the development of content and articles, ensuring that we are ready to go with comment at key legislative milestones. An example would be the run-up to the implementation deadline of the Fourth Money Laundering Directive via the Money Laundering Regulations 2017, or the publication of HMRC Guidance on the new corporate criminal offence of failing to prevent tax evasion and the entry into force of the Criminal Finances Act 2017.

I engage in the initial research and analysis as part of the preparation process for any speaking engagement or event. Working closely with Marketing, I support the delivery of external seminars, speaking engagements and wider networking. I can join the dots in terms of other practice areas – and indeed, within our own criminal team – and monitor who is working on what to provide a full picture. More on relationship building below!

I go beyond the legal research element (which is often undertaken by junior fee-earners) for that particular topic and put myself in the shoes of the conference goer, considering what delegates want to hear about and what it is that Kingsley Napley can bring to the table which is new and interesting.

This comes back to insight and intelligence – what is the next move from the Serious Fraud Office? Large scale litigation or deferred prosecution agreements? What trends are developing in the United States and whether we might see a modelling of Department of Justice practice over here? What next for Legal Professional Privilege protection in internal investigations? Will the Ministry of Justice come off the fence in terms of whether there is a need for wholesale reform of criminal liability for corporates? If so, are we looking to shape the reform of the legal landscape? How will a remark given by a minister at a Select Committee regarding disclosure translate into a new policy or change of direction? What have others in the marketplace said on these issues?

Thought leadership

One example I would like to use is a recent one. I support the international practice group that focuses on extradition, mutual legal assistance and cross-border investigations. In preparing the know-how bundle for a recent meeting I uncovered a (barely reported on) draft piece of legislation – the Crime (Overseas Production Orders) Bill, currently at committee stage in the House of Lords. This will legislate for a new power to secure access to electronic evidence held outside the UK – something that will have significant implications for data privacy and obligations on companies. It is the UK laying the groundwork for co-operation under the US Cloud Act and reflects provisions on the table in Brussels for a European Production Order.

After working alongside a key partner in our international practice on producing blogs and articles, I am now leading on presenting this topic as an external seminar which will include representatives of law enforcement, fair trial NGOs, and a global tech company. I deployed my own network in securing speakers and am currently seeking to expand the invite list beyond our usual suspects in international criminal law, working with our corporate and commercial team to consider interest from any technology clients or those with a large overseas presence. This dynamic approach has given us a head start in terms of building an online presence on this issue and demonstrating our thought leadership capabilities. This in turn allows us to underline our credentials in cross-border investigations and profile our leading practitioners.

Stakeholder engagement

I recently supported team members from our general crime practice in facilitating a meeting with the Law Commission as part of its consultation process on search warrants. Whilst it is sometimes hard to convert a workshop on search warrants with the Law Commission into hard core BD statistics, put this in the light of getting an insight into how the processes relating to search and seizure and "dawn raids" may shape up. It then offers valuable information for the investigations team. It is no longer deemed an academic pursuit, but a valid part of a fee-earner's practice development.

Post-Brexit landscape

On the issue of Brexit I work closely with the firm's "Brexit Legal Group" and work to draw connections across the different practice areas. External sources, monitoring services and updaters provide the baseline updates, so I try to focus on considering the longer-term consequences and additional angles to those already set out. For example, as we look at the impact on the financial services sector and capital markets profiled in the financial news, what might this mean for good governance and the regulatory regime and ultimately investigation and enforcement?

Whilst wading through the analysis of whether the Competition and Markets Authority is prepared for Brexit in terms of state aid and mergers (not actually part of our practice), I focused on the passing reference to the fact that the CMA will have more scope to act independently of the European Commission once the UK leaves the EU. Our cartel team are now reviewing what this might mean for anti-trust enforcement, monitoring the beefing up of CMA resources, and using this as useful insight for when conducting criminal cartel enforcement training with City firm competition teams.

Joining the dots

Whilst I am a core part of the criminal litigation team, the nature of our firm is one of cross-practice – an offering that can encompass regulatory, employment, public law, dispute resolution and the criminal team at any one time, for example. Whilst there is a collaborative culture within the firm, having and taking the time to build relationships across the teams – where there are not always other PSLs – is a key part of what I do. Awareness of and engagement with other teams can deliver benefits in terms of improving knowledge sharing and in turn lay the groundwork for business development.

A key area that exemplifies the cross-practice nature of my work is sexual misconduct in the workplace (or the #MeToo campaign). This is a current area of work where criminal team colleagues are working closely with others across the firm, including Marketing. One of our leading criminal defence partners is due to speak on this topic for a Global Investigations Review (GIR Live) panel in New York in the autumn. Whilst she is a key commentator on this topic and counsel to a number of high profile clients, my role is to ensure she is equipped with a full briefing on our white-collar crime and investigations work, international practice, and anything a US lawyer might want to know about Brexit and cross-border law enforcement! Back at home, I am due to support the roll-out of training on the criminal law aspects of a sexual misconduct investigation to employment teams of City law firms and those within our wider referral network. The team presenting includes senior members of the criminal, employment and regulatory teams, giving a unique insight into the issues and pitfalls in this area.

When canvassing colleagues as to how I can best support them, relationship building and relationship management outside the team was one of the areas identified, with a colleague of mine reporting: "Having someone who can bridge the gaps or know who to call in another team is invaluable". Where we have a panel session coming up on whistleblowing in the business crime sector, I pick up the phone to the employment team. When preparing for a talk to the healthcare sector on recent trends in gross negligence manslaughter, I speak to the regulatory defence team upstairs. Cybercrime group members want to know about class actions for data breach and hacking – off to the dispute resolution team. Controlling and coercive behaviour and domestic abuse – coffee with the family team's PSL. I now understand that session at the very first ARK conference where people talked about the value of know-who as part of know-how!

So back to the theme... the evolving role of the PSL

Some three years into a role that was new for me and new for the team, it has become clear to me that there is no "one size fits all" in terms of this role either within the profession, or indeed my own firm. With effective management support and personal initiative, you become what your team needs you to be. The work that I do and the service that I offer is welcomed and supported by the partnership which in turn endorses my value to the wider department. Ultimately it ensures that I feel like a key member of the team and that my (non-fee earning) contribution is properly recognised.

My work as a PSL: diverse, dynamic and constantly evolving!

Chapter 11: Practice support lawyers in the United States

By Evan J Shenkman, director of KM counsel and research at Ogletree Deakins

Practice/professional support lawyers have been a staple in UK law firms for over two decades, but their penetration into the US legal space is a far more recent phenomenon. When I transitioned from shareholder to PSL in 2011, I was my law firm's first and only PSL (which we call "knowledge management counsel"), and my colleagues at Ogletree Deakins and elsewhere had no idea what I was doing and why.

Fast-forward six years, and I lead a growing team of three PSLs at my firm, a now well-known team of individuals who have revolutionised the way our attorneys practice law. I am also a co-chair of a New York City Practice Support Lawyer's Network that just celebrated its tenth anniversary, and which now boasts 77 members from NYC-based law firms. The PSL profession in the United States is robust and growing, with interesting roles and responsibilities driven by the challenges faced by United States law firms.

In this chapter I will discuss the growth of the profession, the role of PSLs in the US, and how I see the PSL's responsibilities shifting in the years to come. My personal insights will be supplemented with the results of a voluntary PSL experience survey I conducted in July 2018 of over 25 United States-based law firms.

PSLs in the United States

In connection with the preparation of this chapter, I surveyed members of the International Legal Technology Association to inquire about their US-based PSLs. Respondents hailed from 26 US law firms: two firms with fewer than 100 attorneys, five firms with 101-500 attorneys, seventeen firms with 501-1000 attorneys, and two firms with more than 1000 attorneys. The results reflected more than three-quarters of the US firms employed PSLs, with the vast majority of firms (60 per cent) employing between one and five PSLs.[1] What used to be a primarily UK phenomenon has certainly made its way across the pond.

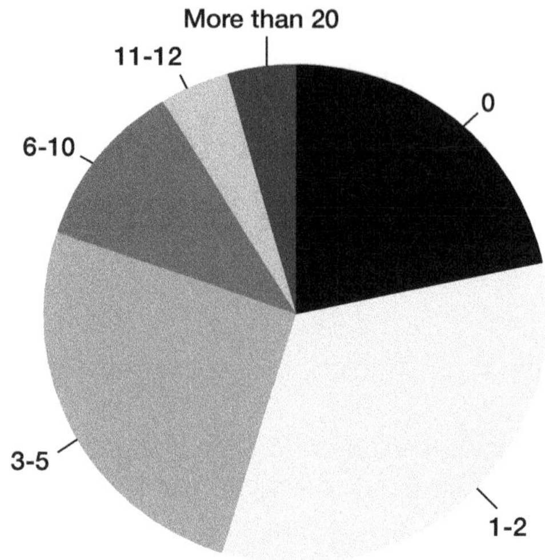

Figure 1: Number of PSLs per firm

The role of PSLs in the United States

When I became a PSL at Ogletree Deakins, the projects I initially focused on were traditional PSL initiatives: development and curation of model documents/forms/checklists/templates; identification of subject matter experts; and working with our team of technicians and developers to roll out enterprise search. As a former shareholder with the firm, I gave those projects credibility: when I recommended a subject matter expert, attorneys trusted my recommendation; when I prepared model templates, attorneys knew they were sound; when I helped build our search platform, I designed it with intimate knowledge of how our attorneys worked and what they needed to find.

Those initial projects were highly successful, and with success came an overwhelming request for PSL assistance. Our PSL team soon grew from one to three PSLs, and so too did our team's responsibilities. Our PSLs now:

- Manage our KM Legal Resource Centre – the firm's home for model documents/templates/samples/practice guides/secondary sources, all organised by legal topic;
- Develop and curate content for the KM Legal Resource Centre and our 50-state survey pages;

- Serve as liaisons to our firm's 37 practice and industry groups, assisting with various KM-related projects (including document repositories, experience surveys, and development and management of group intranet pages);
- Help train our 800+ attorneys to use self-service KM tools and resources;
- Assist lawyers in finding information by suggesting applicable KM resources and search strategies;
- Provide substantive legal updates to our attorneys and practice groups; and
- Investigate and evaluate new vendors in the KM/legal space, including running pilots for artificial intelligence and data analytics software tools and services.

The responsibilities of Ogletree Deakins' PSLs, while diverse, all serve the same important purpose: they help our attorneys work more efficiently, more consistently, and at a higher quality. Our attorneys rarely must start from scratch or bill clients for work already performed elsewhere in our firm; our attorneys can now focus more on legal strategy, and less on minutia and busy-work. Not surprisingly, our PSLs' efforts are cherished both by our attorneys (who love that they can find what they need quickly and easily) and our clients (who see lower bills for higher quality work product). And the services performed by our PSLs (who do not bill their time) are especially critical to support our client engagements on an alternative-fee-arrangement basis.

My PSL experience survey of US law firms reflects similar PSL roles and responsibilities across the spectrum of small and large US firms. The most common PSL responsibility (shared by a whopping 81 per cent of all PSLs) is the development of firm-facing content (exemplars, forms, and models), a classic PSL role. Product testing (77 per cent) earned an especially high value, a point I will come back to in the third part of this chapter. Training on KM resources, and practice group assistance, both were very well-represented (at 72 per cent). Business development and litigation support – roles often handled by separate firm departments at many US firms – were not popular responsibilities for PSLs.

Several survey respondents offered further insight into PSL responsibilities at their firms. Several noted that their PSLs provided document automation assistance, with one noting that: "Our PSL has become the firm's expert in document automation". One stated that process

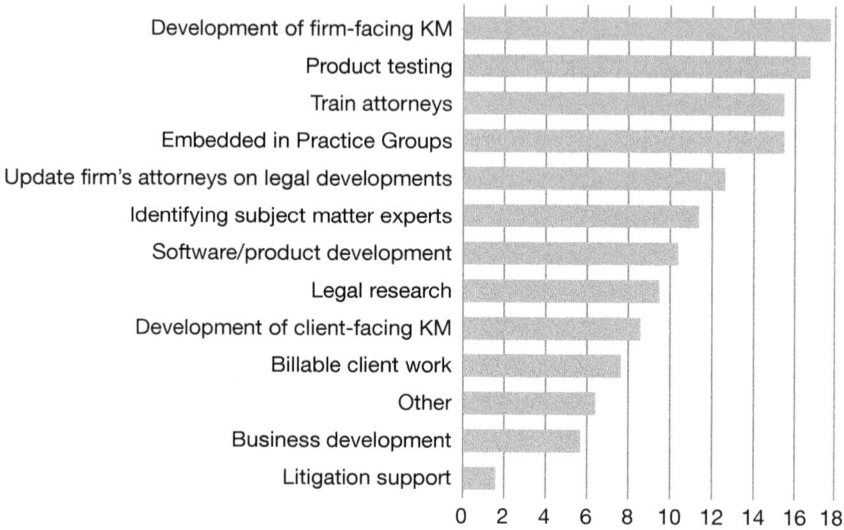

Figure 2: PSL responsibilities

improvement and driving adoption of KM-oriented technology are "important parts" of the PSL role. Another respondent advised that their busy PSLs "help configure intranet pages and evaluate external content sources; help lawyers understand which sources to use for various specific purposes; help with matter profiling values/strategies; help as ambassadors for adoption of KM tools (Knowledge Bank, search, etc.); and help coordinate with client KM teams in situations in which we have those relationships".

The future of PSLs in the United States

I see a bright future for PSLs in the US, and my PSL experience survey of US law firms confirms the good news: more than half of the firms – including one firm who does not currently employ PSLs – plan to grow their US team of PSLs in the next 12 months.[2] My firm is among them. As I will discuss, I credit this anticipated growth to several primary factors: client demand, the rise of alternative fee arrangement engagements, and disruptive innovations in the legal space which are hospitable to PSLs in the US.

Client demands

It has long been said that "the customer is king". This is even more true in the US legal space; today's legal clients are empowered consumers with sophisticated expectations. Beyond price and quality, they now demand efficiency, transparency, value, predictability, innovation, and value-added services. Take, for instance, the following language found in various Requests for Proposals issued to my firm in 2017 and 2018 for US-based legal work:

- How do you leverage your knowledge base to maximise value to the client, including templates, searchable resources, draft policies, AI, etc.?
- Explain your processes and protocols for creating, tracking, and leveraging institutional knowledge.
- How do you systematically reuse work product to lower costs and improve quality?
- How do you identify and tap discrete internal expertise?
- How do you identify knowledge capital, organise it for use, and minimise its loss from personnel turnover?
- How do your knowledge management efforts change the way legal services are delivered?

Law firms lacking credible answers to these questions will cease to win business, and law firms ceasing to win business will cease to be law firms. I see this as good news for PSLs: they are the professionals who prepare templates, resources, and draft policies; they are the professionals who identify and organise knowledge capital; they are the professionals who manage initiatives to create, track, and leverage institutional knowledge. While practicing attorneys could lead these initiatives in lieu of PSLs (and there are several US law firms who follow this model), in my opinion it is less desirable to do so, both in terms of efficiency and focus.[3]

The rise of alternative fee agreement matters

A 2017 survey of chief legal officers conducted by the Association of Corporate Counsel reported that 26 per cent of (global) legal work is structured under an alternative fee arrangement, and almost half of the CLOs polled expected to increase that percentage over the next twelve months. AFAs make up an increasingly important part of my firm's business as well. The rise of AFAs is another harbinger of success for PSLs.

With attorneys unable to make more money by simply billing more hours, initiatives that increase attorney efficiency are at a premium. PSLs enable firms to do more with less, while not compromising quality. These responsibilities include the development and vetting of tools and services that enhance efficiency (e.g. document automation, workflows, process maps, AI, etc.), template and form preparation, and maintenance of systems that help identify the right attorney and right materials for the assignment.

The rise of innovation in legal services

I consider a third driver of the rise in PSLs in the US to be the growth of disruptive innovation in legal services. These include firm-facing innovations (allowing law firms to provide their clients better services) and client-facing innovations (developed by law firms as a revenue-generator or a value-added service for clients). Such innovations include:

- Document automation software (to generate myriad of legal papers with a few keystrokes);
- Artificial intelligence tools (to help prepare drafts of pleadings and discovery, and even evaluate briefs);
- Data analytics tools (to provide insights from date on judges, courts, and opposing counsel);
- Macros and workflow automation software (to quickly complete administrative legal tasks and provide answers);
- Chatbots (to automate questions and answers); and
- Decision tree/expert systems (to provide users with legal guidance following completion of a series of online questions and answers).

Whether firm-facing or client-facing, these disruptive innovations are a boon for PSLs in the US, who play an invaluable role in developing, evaluating, rolling out, training on, and championing such innovations.

I have found my team of PSLs to be ideally suited for these responsibilities because, as former practicing attorneys, they (1) intimately understand attorney needs and workflows and have excellent judgment on whether the innovation is worthwhile; (2) know what firm clients are looking for and would find valuable; (3) have the right subject-matter expertise; (4) tend to be tech-savvy and enjoy reviewing the newest gadgets; (5) can effectively train and champion "lawyer-to-lawyer;" and (6) have the time to lead these explorations and initiatives, having no caseload or business development obligations weighing them down. Of course, while practicing attorneys should be involved to some degree in evaluating and developing such tools and services, PSLs should be tasked with the heavy lifting.

As noted above, more than three-quarters of my PSL experience survey respondents already identified "product testing" as one of their current responsibilities. With the dramatic rise in computing potential and heightened focus on innovation in legal, PSLs can expect this number to go even higher in the years to come.

A few final notes

As mentioned above, I see a bright future for PSLs in the US. Their responsibilities are squarely aligned with the direction that legal is going, both in the drive towards efficiency and AFAs, and the focus on innovation and commoditization of certain legal services. That said, two additional points bear mentioning.

First, PSLs should anticipate that not all seemingly exciting innovations will initially be well-received by practicing attorneys, particularly innovations that could be viewed as jeopardising their status as an indispensable expert, or their ability to bill time. Just as some attorneys initially pushed back against enterprise search ("Those are *my* documents. I don't want them shared!") and against document review software, there will be those who fear that robots are taking over legal. While the firm's CIO or CKO will likely take the lead in defending that claim, PSLs are at the front lines. They should be pre-emptively prepared to explain the value in efficiency; the client demands for innovation; and how attorneys' time is better spent on strategy, analysis, and applying facts to the law, rather than on minutiae and busywork.

Second, while *we* can all agree that PSLs' roles and responsibilities add immeasurable value to law firms, sometimes it is helpful to have that value be *measurable*, especially if someone questions whether a growing team of PSLs makes business sense. Although admittedly difficult, PSLs should continually look for ways to track their worth, whether via usage metrics (on model documents, software tools, intranet page views, etc.); training metrics (number of people trained, topics covered, etc.); RFP successes (if PSLs were involved or their services were promoted); and key accolades received (my team maintains a list of thousands).

Finally, I would like to thank the UK for originating the professional support lawyer position almost thirty years ago. While it took some time to make its way to the US, PSLs are now a robust and valuable part of our practice, and look to remain so for years to come.

References

1. Interestingly, the size of the firm was not a useful indicator of their likelihood to employ PSLs. Among those employing zero PSLs included one small firm (1–20 attorneys), two medium firms (101–250 attorneys), and three large firms

(501–1000 attorneys). That said, the firms with more than ten PSLs each had more than 500 US attorneys.

2. 14 out of 25 respondents, or 56 per cent.
3. Practicing attorneys are extremely helpful contributors to a great number of KM initiatives, but in my experience (1) you need full-time focus on larger-scale KM/PSL projects to be successful, and (2) attorneys are already short on non-billable time after focusing on business development, firm management, reviewing bills, and continuing legal education requirements.

www.ingramcontent.com/pod-product-compliance
Ingram Content Group UK Ltd.
Pitfield, Milton Keynes, MK11 3LW, UK
UKHW021848150926
8657IPUK00005B/146

9 781783 583485